THE ONLY
WRITING BOOK
YOU'LL EVER NEED

*A complete resource for perfecting
any type of writing*

Pamela Rice Hahn

Adams Media
Avon, Massachusetts

Published by Adams Media, an F+W Publications Company
57 Littlefield Street Avon, MA 02322
www.adamsmedia.com

ISBN 10: 1-59337-274-4
ISBN 13: 978-1-59337-274-3
Printed in Canada.

J I H G F E D C B

Contains portions of material adapted and abridged from *The Everything® Writing Well Book* by Pamela Rice Hahn, ©2003, F + W Publications, Inc.

Library of Congress Cataloging-in-Publication Data
Hahn, Pamela Rice.
The only writing book you'll ever need / Pamela Rice Hahn.
p.   cm.
ISBN 1-59337-274-4
1. English language—Rhetoric—Handbooks, manuals, etc. 2. Academic writing—Handbooks, manuals, etc. 3. Business writing—Handbooks, manuals, etc. 4. Letter writing—Handbooks, manuals, etc. I. Title.

PE1408.H2925 2005
808'.042—dc22
2004026349

This publication is designed to provide accurate and authoritative information with regard to the subject matter covered. It is sold with the understanding that the publisher is not engaged in rendering legal, accounting, or other professional advice. If legal advice or other expert assistance is required, the services of a competent professional person should be sought.

—From a *Declaration of Principles* jointly adopted by a
Committee of the American Bar Association and
a Committee of Publishers and Associations

This book is available at quantity discounts for bulk purchases.
For information, please call 1-800-289-0963.

Contents

Chapter 4: Doing Your Research 50

Chapter 5: Basic Essays 62

Chapter 6: Academic Writing 75

Chapter 14: What to Do When You Have Writer's Block 172

Index 180

Introduction

S o this is *The Only Writing Book You'll Ever Need*. This book promises to deliver on a tall order. Polishing and perfecting all of your
writing is an ambitious undertaking, indeed. Before we start extol-
ling the virtues of this small volume—and all of the writing gems you will
glean from it—let's consider why you need this book at all.

Perhaps when you think about writing, newspaper articles, books, or
magazine features come to mind. Or maybe this subject drums up memories of writing high school and college-level research papers. You certainly
will learn about the key principles of journalism and the essentials of academic essays in this book. But good writing isn't a skill relegated only to
the realm of professional journalists, novelists, students, or teachers.

Think about those times when you're doing something as practical
as sending a congratulatory note or preparing a resume to land a new job.
Or maybe you're tackling something more complicated, like applying for
grant funding or crafting a documentation plan for a technical document.
Whatever the case might be, there will always be times in both your personal and professional life where you'll need to step up to the plate and give
writing your best shot.

Good writing is about doing your research, organizing your ideas
properly, and conveying information effectively. Ultimately, good writing

skills equal good communication skills, and good communication is integral to all walks of life.

But good writing also doesn't just happen. Few—if any—writers can produce a perfect piece start to finish in one stream-of-consciousness burst of energy. (And if they tell you they can, they're probably lying.) Writing requires tenacity. It is an ongoing process of putting initial thoughts to paper, then editing, rereading, re-editing, and proofreading.

Be patient as your writing skills develop. At first, the process might seem difficult and frustrating, as you strive to hone your skills and get things right. With practice, however, it will get easier, until you reach a point where you intuitively know where you need to go with your thoughts and how you're going to get there.

Consider this book your basic introduction to planning, researching, organizing, and executing all sorts of writing projects. Until you do reach that point where writing becomes second nature, you'll need guideposts to help you stay on track. As you read this book, you'll encounter simple, distilled instructions as well as a wide range of examples to steer you in the right direction.

Don't be intimidated by writing. The simplicity of this slim guidebook should serve to assuage your fears, by helping you to find ways to hone your focus, stay on topic, develop coherent arguments, and even conquer writer's block when it strikes. And although this truly is *The Only Writing Book You'll Ever Need*, in the sense that it gives you the necessary tools to tackle a variety of tasks, don't stop here. If you intend to pursue any of the writing types detailed in this book further, consult other resources specific to your needs.

Continue reading and practicing, and your writing will continue to improve.

Chapter 1

Laying the Right Foundation

When it comes to writing, the most important thing is getting your point across. Writing is all about communication, and if you want to communicate properly, your messages must be clear and concise. This chapter will help you to understand the basic aspects of effective writing. By using the techniques in this book, your writing will become stronger, and readers will not only have confidence in you as a writer, they'll have more confidence in you as a person, too.

Before you set out to write any sort of message, there are a few decisions you first need to make. Sure, your plan of attack will vary depending on whether you are announcing your engagement, filing a letter of complaint, or writing a massive research paper. Despite the differences, however, *any* effective written message needs to answer the basic questions Who, What, When, Where, Why, and How. It also needs a solid beginning, middle, and end. As you develop the ins and outs of these main objectives, you also need to hone some troubleshooting techniques to avoid common mistakes many writers make. And once you get your ideas out onto the page, don't stop there. Spellcheck isn't the cure for all your woes, so never underestimate the value of editing and proofreading your work.

Addressing the Big Six

All writers, whether seasoned professionals or inexperienced novices, fear the dreaded blank page. Putting your thoughts into writing won't seem so daunting if you clearly define your "big six" questions. The first thing you'll need to do is consider **whom** you're writing for. Determine your audience by asking questions such as these:

- Does your reader already know you?
- Is your reader somebody "in house," or will you be writing to somebody outside your center of influence?
- Is your reader familiar with the topic?
- Will your reader be receptive to what you're writing, or will you need to include any special motivation for continuing?
- Will you need to anticipate and overcome any objections or any ambivalence?

Once you have a firm grasp on who your audience is, it's time to consider **what**, exactly, you're writing about. What kind of information do you plan to disseminate? The information you include and the approach you take will be quite different depending on whether you're writing an information piece about a new company procedure or a short story about survivors of a plane crash.

Don't forget to consider what your readers already know. You don't want to beat a dead horse. When you include too much excess information, you lessen the impact of the new points you're making. Give only as much information as is necessary to provide context.

If your writing involves achieving some practical goal—such as a business report, a letter of dispute, or a social invitation—you naturally need to include **when** the events took or will take place. Likewise, when it comes to fiction, knowing when to set your piece is important. Are you setting the piece in the past? If so, be careful to maintain the illusion of that time period. Even something as innocuous as a tea bag could stick out like a sore thumb if it's not appropriate to the time period. When writing fiction, research the historical context of the period to avoid jarring inconsistencies.

Also don't underestimate the importance of **where** the major events or the action of a story takes place, and how that setting affects the people (or characters, in the case of fiction) who will be involved.

No matter what you're writing, you should always have a grasp on **why** you're doing it. This keeps you focused and on point. No amount of writing preparation will help if you haven't established a clear objective. To establish your objective, focus on the main point you want to convey. If you're writing nonfiction, this should be relatively obvious. Maybe, for instance, your objective is to provide a step-by-step, systematic guide to accomplish a particular task. Then all that's really important is the steps, accompanied by enough information to give it context.

If you're writing fiction, you still need to have an objective. Even if that objective is merely to entertain, every word in your passage should contribute to the end.

Keeping all of the above in mind, your next task is determining **how** you should tell the story:

- How do you plan to get your point across?
- What format will you use?
- Do you want to tell a linear story?
- How do key events in your story occur or progress?
- Do you plan to use flashbacks to establish the history of your characters?

As a preliminary step while you are plotting the course for your writing, make a checklist and check off each of these items as you address them.

The Basic Building Blocks

When broken down into its simplest form, an effective piece of writing is built from three basic parts:

1. A beginning
2. A middle
3. An ending

Don't just jump in and start writing anywhere. Take a few moments to figure out where you want to begin, what you're going to say, and how you're going to wrap things up. Your writing will be much better if you consider these components.

Effective Openings

The general consensus for most fiction today is: "Start with the action." If there are things the reader needs to know about the "beginning" (known as "backstory"), then devices such as flashbacks can be used to supply that information, or it can be worked in as the story moves along. Today's world is fast-paced, and people are not patient. Whether fiction or nonfiction, effective writing should reflect this trait.

Admittedly, beginnings aren't always easy to define. As you'll see in later chapters, you don't get to the opening sentence of a letter until you write the "body." But regardless of its name, an effective opening is one that engages readers from the git-go, so that they hit the ground running, amid the action. Hopefully, all that action will leave the reader wanting to know more.

In formal writing, openings are free of slang or colloquialisms (like "git-go"). When determining how to craft an appealing opening, effective writers should also consider certain things about their readers, such as educational level, gender, and cultural background.

✍ *Formal or Informal?*

If you're writing a quick note to a friend, you're bound to use much different language than you would if you were, say, writing a letter to a lawyer. Tone, diction, and style vary between formal and informal writing. Don't be too formal with your friends, and don't be too informal otherwise.

Middle Matters

When it comes down to it, the middle is where everything substantial happens. The opening may set the tone, but the actual point of your piece will unfold in the middle.

This is where you have the opportunity to fill in background details. Your middle will involve a series of events that slowly culminate in a final, climactic scene. After you reach that point, it's time to wind down.

Wrap It Up

Just as you must be careful to start with the action in your opening, you must also remember to stop where the story ends. Many beginning writers continue writing long after the story is over, rehashing old material. In fiction, your writing is stronger—and has more emotional impact on the reader—if it leaves some things up to the imagination. As long as the major points of the story are wrapped up, you can leave some things unsaid.

Unanswered questions don't make an ending ineffective. Adding too many extras often detracts from the rest of the story. As long as you provide an effective emotional close to your piece, you don't need an answer for everything.

Avoiding Common Mistakes

You now know a little bit about the main ingredients for effective writing. But what sorts of things weaken good writing? Poor grammar and sloppy style, for starters. You may not realize it, but you are judged by what you write. Polishing your grammar, style, and usage not only helps you to convey your message more precisely, it also gives readers confidence that you know what you're talking about.

As you hone your writing skills, keep in mind that writing is an evolving process, not a one-shot deal. Once you get your first draft onto the page, it's time to clean up the words and make sure that you're conveying the proper meaning. The following sections highlight some of the most common mistakes writers make. These are all important things to remember as you edit your work. (Don't worry—this book isn't all negative—in Chapter 2, you'll learn some positive alternatives to help you polish your writing and make it even more engaging.)

Pare It Down

Many writers get caught up in the quest to "sound good," and mistakenly overuse wordy, unnecessary phrases. Try to avoid this pitfall. Here are some of the top offenders you should watch for:

Bad Choices	Good Choices
because of the fact that	since /because
for the period of	for
in many cases	often
in many instances	sometimes
in the nature of	like
the fact that he had not succeeded	his failure

Active and Passive Voice

Simply put, active voice means the subject of the sentence is performing the verb. With a passive sentence, however, the subject is on the receiving end of the verb. Consider the following active example:

The cheerleaders danced to the half-time music.

The subject of the sentence—cheerleaders—is performing the action—dancing to the music. Now look at the following example, which uses passive voice:

The half-time music was accompanied by the dancing of the cheerleaders.

✒ Spotting Passive Voice

There's a simple trick you can use to recognize when the passive voice is being used. If the word "by" is used in the sentence to indicate who is performing the action, it's probably written in a passive voice construction.

As you can see, the music isn't actually doing anything. The cheerleaders are still doing the dancing, but the action of the sentence has shifted. When you construct a sentence using passive voice, the subject of the sentence receives the action of the verb instead of performing it.

Unnecessary Adjectives

Adjectives modify nouns or pronouns. When used properly, they add a great deal of depth to writing. When used improperly, however, adjectives make writing seem unprofessional and stilted. Consider this example:

> **The elderly man picked up his ugly, rusty old razor and began to shave his craggy, wrinkled face.**

As you can see, too many adjectives in a sentence can make the reader stumble. Break up your adjectives and intersperse them within a number of sentences; bite-sized nuggets are much easier for the reader to swallow and digest. Better yet, try to stretch out the description, so you're not relying entirely on adjectives:

> **The old man picked up his razor. It was rusty, but it was all he had. He lathered up the soap and applied it to his face, covering up the wrinkles and stubble in preparation for his shave.**

Excess Adverbs

Adverbs are words that modify verbs, adjectives, or other adverbs. They can convey degree, manner, number, place, or time. Adverbs can ask questions; they can also modify entire clauses in a sentence, like the word *however* does in the next paragraph.

Most adverbs end in *–ly,* such as *quickly, angrily,* and *goodheartedly. Who, what, when, where,* and *why* are all adverbs, too, and they're good ones to use. If adverbs appear too frequently in your writing, however, try to cut them out.

The adverbs listed below are often overused in written English—use them sparingly.

- Accordingly
- Also
- Anyhow
- Consequently
- Otherwise

- Still
- Then
- Therefore
- Yet

Don't worry—it's relatively easy to work around these words. Simply restructure your sentence and try to do away with the adverb.

Noun-Pronoun Agreement

Pronouns are words that take the place of nouns. They're useful because they are short and concise, and they cut down on needless repetition.

Common English Pronouns

Subject	Object	Possessive
I	me	my
you	you	your
he	him	his
she	her	her
it	it	its
we	us	our
they	them	their
who	whom	whose

Because a pronoun is used in place of a noun, it must have a noun to relate to. This is why some grammar teachers stress that you should never start a sentence with *it*.

It ran the length of the track before it returned to the stable.

What exactly is *it*? How can you tell? You might be able to gain an inference from the sentence; after all, how many things will run a track and then return to the stable? However, this creates work for the reader, and any time you make a reader think, you run the risk of losing him or her along the way. A much better choice would be:

> The horse ran the length of the track before it returned to the stable.

Be careful with pronoun agreement. A pronoun must relate to a noun in terms of number and gender. Never use *it* when you actually mean *them*, or vice versa, and never use *her* for a male or *him* for a female. The pronoun *they* should never take the place of either *he* or *she*; likewise, *them* should never be substituted for *him* or *her*.

Ambiguous Pronoun Usage

When pronouns are used improperly, sentence meaning is often ambiguous. If only two people are talking, a male and a female, the pronoun usage should be obvious. But with two people of the same sex, or a group, it's often confusing. Consider the following example:

> "How is your shift going?" Matthew asked David, sitting down at his desk and running his fingers through his hair.

At whose desk did Matthew sit? Matthew's or David's? Moreover, whose hair did Matthew run his fingers through? Matthew's or David's? At first glance, it might seem obvious what's truly going on in the sentence, namely that Matthew sits at his own desk and runs his fingers through his own hair while he converses with David. Still, the pronoun usage in the sentence is far from specific. A much better sentence construction would be:

> Matthew sat down at his desk and ran his fingers through his hair. "How is your shift going?" he asked David.

✍ Sentence Structure Tip

When writing, keep your sentences as concise as possible. Normally, this means "short," but don't oversimplify your sentences if you're trying to make a specific point. A sentence should be as long as it needs to be—and no longer.

Subject and Verb Agreement

The verbs you use must always agree with the subject to which they correspond. For example, you would say: He goes to the store every Tuesday or they go to the store every Tuesday.

Note that two singular subjects, when acting together, will take a plural verb. For example: Sam and Bill go to the store every Tuesday.

Verb Tense Agreement

There are three basic tenses in the English language: the past, the present, and the future. In most writing, you will use the past tense, especially when you are describing events that have already occurred.

✍ Sentence Length

Always vary the length of your sentences. Don't use a lot of short sentences unless you're trying to establish a scenic objective, such as suspense, or a sense of immediacy. It's better to stagger sentences so that you have longer ones broken up by shorter ones. This creates variety and keeps things interesting for the reader.

The past and future tenses have further divisions, too. For example, forms of the past tense are past progressive, past perfect, and past perfect progressive tenses. You can talk about events that occurred in the past, and you can also talk about events that occurred before those events. If you aren't careful about using these tenses properly, things could get pretty confusing. Improperly constructed sentences also look silly, and this could comprise your credibility as a writer.

Consider the following example:

> **Mandy walked into the bathroom, picked up the towel, and begin to dry her hair. When she was done, she put the towel back where it was.**

In both sentences, the verbs are in the immediate past tense. Yet, the sentence is referring to where towel was *before* the other events took place. Therefore, a slightly different tense is needed:

> **Mandy walked into the bathroom, picked up the towel, and began to dry her hair. When she was done, she put the towel back where it had been.**

Now, the verbs clearly show that Mandy put the towel back in the place it had been before she picked it up. Pay careful attention to your verb tenses—proper verb tenses make things much clearer.

✍ Reining in Run-Ons

Some people just fall into the habit of making their sentences run on too long, without any breaks in their ideas. As a general rule of thumb, a sentence should only have one point. Sometimes you can add on another point as a subclause, but if it gets any more complicated than that, consider breaking the sentence up into smaller bits.

Proper Punctuation

Punctuation is an important part of writing. Punctuation marks tell us when sentences end and when new ones begin. They break up the grammar of the sentence so that we can quickly understand the meaning. They give a context to the words we use. Make sure you understand how to use the following punctuation marks properly, and watch for errors as you edit and proofread your work.

Serial Comma

Historically, the serial comma was used to separate all the nouns when more than two are listed in a sentence. A modern convention omits the last comma from the series, leaving the conjunction to tie them together. Unless you're writing to magazine, newspaper, or Web page guidelines that suggest otherwise, whenever you have three or more nouns listed in a sentence, use a serial comma to separate all of them, including the noun preceding the conjunction. For example:

> **Tom, Dick, and Harry are my friends.**

Don't think that you only have to worry about sentences that include *and*. Serial commas work with other conjunctions, too:

> **I'm going to the store with Tom, Dick, Sue, or Harry.**

✍ What Are Serial Semicolons For?

When your writing involves lists of long, compound phrases instead of simple nouns, or compound phrases in which internal commas are present, using serial commas to separate each entry can get complicated. In these instances, consider using serial semicolons instead.

Exclamation Points

An exclamation point is a very powerful form of punctuation. It should be used sparingly, however, because overuse clouds writing and makes it look amateurish. Use exclamation points sparingly. If you constantly use exclamation points in dialog, the results look absurd:

> **Bob picked up the newspaper. His picture was on the cover! He picked up the phone and quickly dialed his girlfriend. "Bess! You'll never believe it!"**
> **"I know, I know! I saw it!" she said excitedly over the phone. "You must be so thrilled! Congratulations!"**

Now consider a much cleaner version:

> **Bob picked up the newspaper and found that his picture was on the cover. He quickly picked up the phone and dialed his girlfriend. "Bess! You'll never believe it."**
>
> **"I know, I know! I saw it," she said excitedly over the phone. "You must be so thrilled. Congratulations!"**

In this second instance, the emotion of the situation is still conveyed, but it is more controlled and directed—and the characters sound far less maniacal, too.

Chances are, with some thought and careful editing, you'll refine that passage even further and eliminate most of the exclamation points (and the adverb "excitedly"). A more specific verb, such as "exclaimed," would better express the intended emphasis.

✍ Be Mindful of Readership Level

No matter what you write, always keep your readership level in mind. If you're writing for a group of children, you'll want to use simple concepts and simple language to convey your meaning. If, on the other hand, you're writing for academics, your language will be aimed differently. When you're not sure who your readership will be, err on the side of caution and assume a readership level of about seventh to tenth grade.

As a rule of thumb, use exclamation points sparingly in dialog. And never, ever use it in prose or narrative unless you're sure it's necessary.

En and Em Dashes

Although these names may sound funny, there's a logical explanation for them. An en dash (–) is shorter than an em dash (—). This harks back to the days of printing presses; an en dash was simply a dash as long as the letter *n*, and an em dash was one as long as an *m*—or roughly double the length of an *n*.

✍️ Paragraph Structure Tip

Limit your paragraphs to one point or idea. Rather than introduce multiple ideas in the course of one paragraph, break up the ideas and present them in individual paragraphs. This makes it easier for readers to follow your message.

En dashes are most often used to break off ranges of numbers. Em dashes are used for emphasis, to break up parts of a sentence—like when you're including something aside from your main point—but don't do it very often. Otherwise, like exclamation points, em dashes lose their emphasis and become distracting.

Apostrophes: Possessive Pronouns Versus Contractions

Many people get confused about the proper construction of possessive pronouns and contractions, so they end up using apostrophes incorrectly in writing all the time. Consider the following example:

> **Wrong:** The book is her's.

> **Correct:** The book is hers.

Never use an apostrophe to indicate possession with a pronoun. This includes *it's* and *its*—the possessive pronoun *its* should never have an apostrophe; the apostrophe is used only for a contraction. Likewise, *whose* and *who's* also often cause confusion. *Who's* is the contraction of *who is* (as in "Who's coming to dinner?") and whose is the possessive pronoun (as in "At whose house will we be meeting for lunch?").

An apostrophe *s* is only used to indicate possession or contraction, not to make a noun plural.

> **Whose dog is that?**
> **That's Sara's dog.**

If the word with the apostrophe is a contraction, it can be stretched out to its full version. Spelled out in full, the sentence would read, "That is Sara's dog," because the apostrophe *s* takes the place of the *is*.

However, the apostrophe *s* following *Sara* is a possessive adjective.

If it's a possessive apostrophe, you should be able to reconstruct the sentence using the word *of* to indicate possession. (In the example on page 14, for instance, you could rewrite *That's Sara's dog* to read *that's the dog of Sara*.) If you can't do either of those things, then it's probably used with a plural noun that should not take an apostrophe in the first place.

✍ Gender Balance

Never use him or her exclusively when referring to people in general, because you're excluding approximately half of the population. While some people use so-called "gender neutral" words like they or them as inoffensive catch-alls, those are grammatically incorrect. (You can't use a plural pronoun as a replacement for a singular one.) It's best to use he or she to remedy this problem. If this starts to look a little clunky when used frequently in text, simply alternate, using him in one passage, and her in the next.

Proofreading Skills

Once you put your initial thoughts to paper and reworked your draft, you still need to ensure that your writing is free of spelling mistakes and grammatical errors. It's always helpful to have someone else read over your work, just to give it a fresh set of eyes. But even at times when no one else is available, you can still do the job yourself. Just put your writing aside for a few days, to gain objectivity. You'll be more likely to notice mistakes when you're fresh.

Beyond Spellcheck

With the proliferation of computers and word-processing programs, many people have come to rely on technology to tell them whether or not words are spelled correctly. For most, running a spellcheck is about as far as proofreading a document goes. As long as error messages don't pop up along the way, people assume everything is spelled correctly.

✎ Proofreading Tricks

Looking for other tricks to help you catch mistakes in your writing? Try reading what you've written out loud, slowly. The "out loud" part is essential because you'll pick up on instances where you stumble over awkward words and phrases or grammatical errors. Scanning your text backward is also helpful, because it breaks the flow of the content and helps you to focus on nitty-gritty errors instead.

Remember, a spellchecker is nothing more than a lexicon—a list of words. A spellcheck error message is only a notification that the computer doesn't recognize the word after it compares the word to its internal lists. Sometimes, the computer will offer suggestions, but this is simply based on similarities between your word and the list of words it uses to compare.

✎ Cultural Differences in Language

If you're working cross culturally—that is, there are a wide variety of cultures in your market—be particularly careful of the words you choose and how you write. Some words take on unique meanings in certain geographic areas, or mean something completely different in another language. "Slang" meanings can be quite different from actual meanings, and this could also cause you lots of embarrassment if you choose the wrong words. Use colloquialisms carefully in casual writing or fiction, and avoid them altogether in formal writing.

Don't let spellcheckers lull you into a false sense of security. Computers can't actually think, so they don't pick up on subtle linguistic nuances, such as differences between homonyms. (Homonyms are words that sound alike, but are spelled differently and have different meanings, such as *their, there,* and *they're*; or *rain* and *reign*.)

Grab a Good Dictionary

Whenever you're proofreading, get into the habit of reaching for your dictionary. A dictionary will tell you about proper spelling *and* proper usage. Chances are, if you take a few seconds to look up a word and read the definition, you probably won't ever have a problem with that word again. If you use the Internet, there are a great number of dictionaries available online, such as Merriam-Webster Online at *www.m-w.com*. However you do it, it's worth taking a few extra seconds to make certain that you're using the proper word, and the proper spelling.

Use a Thesaurus Carefully

A thesaurus can be a great resource for expanding your vocabulary. It provides lists of synonyms, or words that have similar meanings, to help you say things a little differently. Many word-processing programs have a thesaurus included, and you can also find them on the Internet (Merriam-Webster Online has one, in addition to its dictionary).

Never assume, however, that the words in a thesaurus are interchangeable. The words you'll find will be similar, but their meanings won't be identical. Before you use a word you find in a thesaurus, look it up in the dictionary to determine its actual meaning. If you don't, you might inadvertently use a word that doesn't quite carry the precise meaning you intend.

Chapter 2

Engaging Your Reader

All good writers should have a solid bag of stylistic tricks to draw on so they can craft engaging prose. In this chapter, you'll find a variety of techniques you can use to make sure your readers remain entertained. Remember all of those stylistic pitfalls from Chapter 1? Here, you'll find some useful remedies. Who needs unnecessary adjectives or excess adverbs when you've got descriptive nouns and active verbs ready to take their place?

As you fine-tune your skills, you'll develop your own sense of style, voice, and rhythm, and your writing will have more impact on readers. "Impact" describes how well you're getting your point across. Are you using the proper words? Is your voice on target? Is your writing well paced? All of these things dictate the effect your story will have—and the level of impression your work leaves on your readers' minds and imaginations.

Spicing Up Your Words

Although good writing isn't just about making things sound pretty, it sure keeps things interesting when the words have a nice ring to them. The following techniques will liven up your writing and make it more detailed.

Using Descriptive Nouns

A noun is a word that designates a person, place, or thing. Nouns can be simple and generic, like *book*, or they can be more descriptive, like *romance, mystery,* or *thriller.* The more descriptive your nouns, the more vivid your writing will be.

Take the noun *dog*, for instance. *Dog* is a nondescript noun that only conveys a limited, basic meaning. But *Chihuahua, terrier,* and *dachshund* . . . now those are more descriptive—and, therefore, more effective—choices. Such words paint a recognizable picture in the reader's mind, and that sort of vividness makes your writing livelier and more specific. Wherever possible, choose colorful nouns rather than generic ones.

Choosing Action Verbs

Action verbs are verbs that describe action, as opposed to verbs that describe a state of being. *To act, to sing, to dance,* and *to write* are all examples of action verbs. At the opposite end of the spectrum is the verb *to be*, which is relatively flat and lifeless because it merely describes a state.

In crafting your writing, choose verbs that show action. Sometimes, you will want to use weaker verbs like *to be* in order to establish your setting and mood. The verb *to be* is also important because it serves as a conjunctive verb that gets used in complex constructions. For example:

> **Jessica is singing a song.**
> **Martin is writing a play.**

In these cases, the word *is*, a conjugated form of the verb *to be*, is also used as a linking verb that completes the conjugation of the other verbs *to sing* and *to write*. Beyond such instances, however, use inactive verbs sparingly. Verbs that show activity are always more effective.

There is one exception: Don't make a habit of using action verbs to attribute dialog when characters are speaking. Too many action verbs in dialog attributions actually slow conversation flow. In dialog, what's important are the words being said. Attribution tags should be as simple as possible, and not every line of dialog needs to have a tag. When two characters are conversing, it is usually obvious which character is speaking. Attribution becomes necessary primarily when there are long passages of dialog, to help the reader understand along the way.

Adding Similes, Metaphors, and Analogies

Similes, metaphors, and analogies are similar in nature. Each is used to paint a picture with words. A simile is the most literal and straightforward; it uses the word *like* or *as* to make a comparison:

> He's crazy like a fox.
> He's as crazy as a fox.

These sentences aren't meant to be taken literally—they're figurative statements designed to add depth to the description.

A metaphor sits at the opposite end of the spectrum. It states that one thing is something else. A metaphor creates striking visual impact for your reader. Its meaning is still figurative, but a metaphor causes you to read between the lines. Consider the following example:

> Don't pull my leg.

Nobody's leg is actually being pulled. It simply means, "Be serious with me; don't joke around!" But the metaphor is, for whatever reason, that you're pulling on someone's leg by not telling the truth.

At the beginning of this discussion on metaphors, a metaphor was actually used: "A metaphor sits at the opposite end of the spectrum." If you think about it, a metaphor can't actually sit anywhere—it's a thought, not something concrete. That sentence was a figurative metaphor, but it did its job conveying the meaning. That's how a good metaphor should be—invisible to the reader unless he or she is looking for it.

In between simile and metaphor is analogy. An analogy is usually longer than a simile or metaphor because you're using it to compare one situation to another. That's the big difference—when you use an analogy, you are directly comparing two things. A simile is like a very short analogy; an analogy may use *like* or *as*, but your comparison can be as much as a paragraph. With analogy, you provide more detail.

✍ Quick Recall

You can remember what a simile is by remembering that it states a similarity. A metaphor, on the other hand, goes the extra distance and actually says that something has certain characteristics. Both are important tools in the writer's toolbox.

To use analogy, just take a simile or metaphor and elaborate upon it. Stretch it out, and use the example to illustrate the point you're trying to make. Use it when a simile or metaphor won't establish enough of the meaning you're trying to convey.

When Not to Be Literal

Beyond similes, metaphors, and analogies, there are other literary techniques you can use to incorporate figurative descriptions into your writing.

Allusion: When you create an allusion, you are pointing out the similarities between two concepts on a basic level, without going into too much depth.

Hyperbole: Hyperbole is overexaggeration for the purpose of emphasis. The statement "There has to be a six foot mountain of snow out there!" might not be very factual, but it delivers a clear mental image of the amount of snow and the character's reaction to it.

Personification: In personification you give an inanimate object the qualities of a human. You can also do the same with insects and animals.

Understatement: Understatement basically is the opposite of hyperbole. When using it, you are underplaying the fact you are presenting, making it seem less important than it actually is.

These devices will come up most often in fiction writing, but they can also be used in nonfiction writing to emphasize a point.

Developing a Sense of Voice

The voice of your piece is determined by how you plan to tell the story. When establishing a voice for your writing, ask yourself several questions:

- Who should the reader perceive as the author, and what type of tone is the author taking with the reader?
- Should the author of the piece be invisible to the reader? If so, then first-person pronouns, such as I or we, should not be used.
- Should the reader feel as if the author is speaking directly to him or her? If so, use the second person pronoun "you" a lot.
- Should both the author and the reader be invisible? Then only third-person pronouns should be used, with no reference to I or you. This is the way most novels are written, with clear boundaries separating the reader from the piece, while also keeping the author invisible.

In fiction—novels in particular—third person voice is often used. The author is invisible and unknown, and the reader isn't addressed. In many nonfiction books, as in the one you're now reading, the author and the reader are both acknowledged as active participants. Both types of writing reflect a different voice, because each has a different objective.

In a novel or short story, you are trying to paint a picture using words, giving the reader something to enjoy. In nonfiction, frequently you are conveying information or expertise, so the use of first-person pronouns can be completely acceptable. For much the same reason, second-person pronouns are acceptable, too, because you're often speaking directly to the reader.

✍ First Person Has Its Limits

First-person voice won't work for stories in which you want to have scenes that take place away from the main character. Keep that in mind before you choose a particular voice.

First-person novels are a different story. The voice is often that of the protagonist, although there are some exceptions. Many people would agree that Sherlock Holmes was the protagonist of those stories, but the first-person narrator was Dr. Watson.

First-person writing gives a direct involvement with the reader because the reader is allowed to climb directly inside the head of the narrator.

Working on Hooks, Pacing, and Rhythm

A "hook" is an interesting part of your story that grabs the reader's attention, whether it be a piece of dialog, a description, or anything else. With practice, you can quickly become adept at writing them.

The trick to a strong hook is to start with the action. How you actually start will depend on your objective and on your viewpoint. When you're starting a story, don't spend a lot of time establishing setting or character. You want the reader to want to read your story; too much information at the beginning is a sure way to lose the reader's interest. Start with the action, and you'll pique the reader's curiosity. You can work in setting and character details later, once you've whetted the reader's appetite for more.

With nonfiction, whether writing a technical piece or a letter, there's a temptation to provide "backstory" details before getting to the point. Writing that states its objective (the action) up front is more effective.

As good as a story's hooks can be, they won't carry the entire piece. Writers need to work hard at pacing the flow of the entire story. Pacing is simply the time you take to convey your information in your writing. If you do it at a slow, leisurely pace, you will create a different emotional impact than if you follow the action crisply and closely.

The pace of your writing will also depend on the kind of manuscript you're writing. Different types of stories, books, and scenes will carry different requirements when it comes to pacing. If you're setting up scenes, a slow pace is probably effective. As previously mentioned, in a high-action scene, you want events to unfold quickly to keep the reader at a high emotional level of involvement.

The concept of rhythm can apply to many parts of your writing. On a sentence level, the way the words fit together and how they sound can create a certain poetic cadence. But rhythm goes much deeper.

Short sentences convey urgency. Look! The shorter the sentence, the more urgent the feeling. Incomplete sentence fragments, like the one you just read, quicken the pace, too. If you are writing a dramatic scene, short sentences hurry the reader along. Longer sentences create a laid-back feeling. Consider the following example.

> **Jessica gasped as she watched the man walking toward the house. She ducked low behind the hedge, being careful not to be seen, and tried to remain quiet so as not to attract the man's attention. She thought that she could see the hint of a knife in his hand, but she wasn't entirely sure.**

Now, look at this:

> **Jessica gasped. She shifted her position, covertly cowering behind the hedge. She watched the unshaven man approach. She was close enough to catch his scent. It wasn't pleasant. She could see a glint of shiny metal. Was he holding a knife? She couldn't tell.**

Which example made you feel more tense? You get the picture. The rhythm of the scene is dictated by the objective you're trying to accomplish—choose your rhythm accordingly.

Show Your Story, Don't Tell It

Beginning writers are often admonished for this. If you tell the story instead of showing how it unfolds, you risk boring the reader. Remember, editors are readers, too, and if you're looking to submit something for publication, you'll never even get it through the front door if it's boring. Maintaining your reader's interest level should always be first and foremost in your mind. The most effective way to engage your reader is by showing the story. Consider the following example of bad storytelling:

> Greg went to the store. While there, he bought a gallon of milk. On his way out, he ran into his grade school teacher and spoke with her for a moment before proceeding on his way.

Not very interesting, is it? It's flat and lifeless, and serves only as a grocery list (no pun intended) of what happened. Not only that, it robs you of the opportunity to involve your reader in the action and convey little bits of information about the characters in your story.

Now, look at what it's like when you show the action:

> Greg pulled open the door and stepped through. A slightly musty smell assaulted his nostrils as he walked into the old corner store and faced the high, cramped shelves. The scuffed floor creaked under his weight as he walked over to the ancient milk cooler. The clerk's eagle eyes never left him, giving the impression the clerk thought he might try to stuff a dusty can of peas into his coat pocket.
>
> Greg opened the cooler and picked up a pint of milk, being careful to check the expiration date. Satisfied that it was relatively fresh, he took it up to the front counter.
>
> As he was counting out change, the door opened. He glanced over and recognized Mrs. McGillicuddy, whom he hadn't seen since grade school. She had hardly changed a bit, despite the usual signs of aging. He smiled at her and called her by name.
>
> She looked toward him, with a blank smile. Suddenly, recognition lit her eyes. "Greg!" she exclaimed, smiling broadly.
>
> Greg smiled back. "How on earth did you ever recognize me? It must be thirty years since I've seen you."
>
> The elderly lady smiled mysteriously. "I always remember my star pupils."

Did the second version make you feel more involved? Did the small corner store feel more immediate and real? Did you find it more interesting?

While this example isn't exactly a literary masterpiece, it does demonstrate what it felt like to be in the store at that particular moment, which the first example failed to do. It also raised questions about the characters and probably made you want to learn more about them.

Using Sensory Description

In the preceding description, the words musty and dusty evoked the reader's sense of smell. Hearing was also engaged through the creaking floor, and sight was used, too. Think of times when you've become so involved in what you're reading you've actually felt the sensory cues being described. Have you ever been reading a story about a blizzard and felt a chill, despite the searing, mid-summer heat? That's the power of the mind.

The combination of all of the senses makes the reader feel as if he or she is standing alongside the characters, watching what happens as the events transpire, which creates a feeling of involvement. Get into the habit of involving the senses in your writing:

Touch: What texture do objects have? Is the chair hard, or soft and plush? Show how the surroundings feel to your characters.

Smell: What do your characters' surroundings smell like? Fresh? Smoky? Sweet? Acrid?

Sight: What kinds of things do the characters see? When describing surroundings, use visual words that convey the color, shape, and other physical attributes of objects to show the reader what is being seen instead of just telling the reader that something is within sight.

Hearing: What kinds of sounds are being made in the surroundings? If your characters are at the waterfront, can they hear waves lapping against the wharf? Can they hear seagulls calling?

Taste: Unless it is something that directly relates to the story, you may not want to describe exactly how a meal tastes to the character. However, small clues about things that involve the character's taste buds can help draw the reader into the action.

✍️ The Setting Is Secondary

Remember, the setting of your scene should be secondary to what's actually transpiring in the story. You should use the senses to complement your scene, not construct it.

As you're writing a scene, try to use at least two of the senses to make your reader feel like he or she is participating in the story. The more you can use, the better, but don't force it.

Crafting Effective Transitions

Whenever you move along from one scene to the next, you need to use a transition. After all, you can't expect your reader to spend every moment with a character from the time the character wakes up to the time he or she goes to bed. You need to select which scenes you wish to include, and then use transitions to make the gaps seem logical.

A transition is simply a way of notifying the reader that a passage of time has occurred. The trick is to make it clear to the reader that it's happened so the reader won't feel lost as he or she continues reading. Following are common transition forms you can use to shift time in your story.

Hiatus: This is a series of blank lines separating paragraphs. The initial paragraph after the hiatus begins in the new time period, and the reader automatically knows the shift in time is occurring because of the "break" in the page. If your hiatus falls at the end of a page, you need to indicate the break with a series of three centered asterisks. Be careful not to overuse this device; the hiatus should only be used when there is a clear break between scenes.

One-liners: When a series of actions that aren't integral to the story line occurs, you can quickly gloss over them in one sentence, just to fill the reader in on what has transpired. If nothing important has happened, just sum everything up and continue.

Time phrases: Use stock phrases like "the next day," "that afternoon," "the next morning," or broader passages of time, such as "the next month," to convey elapse of time. Use these sparingly, as too many will make it seem like you're telling the reader instead of showing.

Scenic transitions: You can create an entire, but short, scene to convey that time has passed. Using this type of transition lets you elaborate upon your setting and deliver more information about your character. Rather than glossing over the waiting period, scenic transition allows reader identification to occur.

Dialog: When your characters speak about doing something, it's not much of a logical jump for the reader to expect that they actually start doing it. Dialog transitions are economical because the reader is quickly carried along with the flow of the story without even realizing that a transition has occurred.

Habits: Habitual actions can also signify the passing of time. They also tend to be economical, conveying the time passage in very few words. You can use all sorts of habits—smoking cigarettes, drinking cups of coffee, chewing sticks of gum, or even reading a certain number of magazines to signify time passage effectively.

For maximum effect, learn how to use all of these techniques. The more you mix and match, the more varied and interesting your writing will be.

Such Style

Throughout this chapter, there's been lots of talk about techniques you can use to craft engaging writing that captures reader interest. When you boil it down, all of this stuff about voice, pacing, rhythm, and sensory description relates to a writer developing his or her own unique sense of style. But what, exactly, is style? Style is an amorphous thing. Many writers don't even realize they have a particular style; they just write. But there's something unmistakable about their writing nevertheless—something you just can't miss.

As you read a particular author's work, you get familiar with his or her writing style. Stephen King, for example, has a very different style from Danielle Steele, and not just because each author writes about different subjects.

Many beginning writers think that they can bend the rules or do whatever they like when writing, and simply call it their "style." True enough, as your writing experience grows and you become more adept at the rules, you're allowed certain liberties. But this is only because you understand the essentials of good writing well enough to know where and when you can bend them. So, in your early days, be attentive to the way things should be done, and worry about breaking the mold later.

✍ Formal Versus Informal Writing

The rules for informal writing are somewhat relaxed—you can get away with slang, for instance. Formal writing is different. Formal writing is often used in academic situations where the audience has a professional background. As such, you shouldn't use colloquialisms or other informal conventions. Stick to traditional punctuation styles and grammar usage. But be careful not to sound too presumptuous—just because a setting is formal, that doesn't mean you should use only big words.

Ultimately, however, style is much more than sticking to the basic rules. Style is about how you put your words together into sentences, your sentences together into paragraphs, and so on. As you develop your writing style, it will turn into your personal "voice." With practice, the way you transform your thoughts into words will become almost habitual and completely natural to you.

Chapter 3

Letters and E-mails

Descriptive techniques and literary devices are all well and good, but writing encompasses more than just those finer points of creativity. For most of us, writing serves a utilitarian purpose—it is integral to our daily communication. What better place to start than with day-to-day writing we do all the time? In this chapter, you'll tackle common types of letters, from letters of complaint or dispute, to invitations and thank-you notes. You'll also get a feel for the finer points of electronic communication.

If you dread putting your thoughts to paper and think a quick phone call is your easy out, think twice. Phone calls aren't always the most practical or efficient course of action. You don't want to get caught in a frustrating game of phone tag, and there are also many occasions when you need to document incidents in writing. On a personal level, letters are also less embarrassing and emotional, and they give you the opportunity to be more considerate by providing people with pertinent details (dates, times, etc.) that are more difficult to keep track of through a phone message alone.

The Letter-Planning Process

Writing a letter is like any other form of writing. It's important to take the steps to organize (or outline) your work. Good planning streamlines the editing process and saves you time in the long run.

✍ Business Letter Etiquette

The personalized stationery you got for Christmas may be lovely, but it isn't appropriate for formal or business-related correspondence. Business letters should always be typed, using standard 8½" x 11" paper—it's easier to file. Although it's tempting to get crazy with fonts, use Courier New, Garamond, or Times New Roman in 12 point.

For instances when you have a good idea of what you need to say in a letter, writing your thoughts out in a stream-of-consciousness flow might be quicker than actually preparing an outline. Once that's done, all you need to do is edit your letter before you print it out.

At other times, you might need to brainstorm. First, write out those things you believe you should include. Don't be overly judgmental—just list anything that comes to mind. Next, arrange the items in order of importance, highlighting those ideas that are the most essential.

As you learned in Chapter 1, unless you're writing fiction, what you write should follow a linear progression and have a recognizable beginning, middle, and end.

Essentially, the parts of a formal letter include:

1. **Salutation and introductory comments:** "Dear <name>" is the salutation. The first introductory lines of your letter should set the tone and convey what the letter will be about.
2. **Body:** This is the part that expounds on your message.
3. **Ending sentiment and complimentary close:** The ending sentiment encompasses the final sentences in your letter, with the intent of leaving a positive impression. The complimentary closing is your parting phrase, such as *Sincerely.*

In most cases, an informal letter or note will still contain the same parts. The tone is just less rigid, and you can use more familiar or casual language, such as a complimentary closing like *With Love* or *Hugs*.

✍ Handwritten Notes

Although business letters should never be handwritten, it's a wonderful idea to handwrite personal communications. In these days of e-mails, handwritten letters on note cards are often a welcome surprise.

Complaint and Dispute Letters

From time to time, we all find ourselves embroiled in situations where complaint letters are necessary, whether for billing or disputes, order delays, or incorrect shipments. An effective complaint letter gets results because it provides the recipient with something that demands (literally and figuratively) attention. A complaint letter that effectively presents your grievances in a tactful, logical way is far more effective.

Sample Complaint Letters

Personal Complaint Letter

(Date)

Dear Mrs. Jones,

I'm writing to you about concerns my wife and I have about your dog. Whenever our children play in our yard, your dachshund's barking has us concerned that should your dog ever escape from your fenced-in yard, it would pose a threat to our children. We should set up a meeting within the next week to discuss this situation.

Sincerely,

Paul Smith

Keep in mind that your complaint letter has a better chance of getting resolved if it's written politely. Any letter that you write while angry should serve only as a first draft that allows you to vent your frustration. Once you've had a chance to distance yourself from your anger, edit the letter so that it is worded in a way that will help you reach your objective.

When writing service disputes or merchandise complaints, provide supporting documents, including photocopies of dated receipts, place of purchase, product description, model and serial numbers.

Whenever possible, direct your letter to a specific person. A letter sent to a "department" might be shuffled from desk to desk for a long time before somebody researches and responds to your complaint—or worse, ignores your letter altogether.

Formal Complaint Letter

(Date)

Dear Presto Software Company Customer Service Supervisor:

I returned a software package to your company almost a month ago and I have yet to receive the promised replacement for those damaged goods.
Supporting documents you'll find attached with this letter are:

A copy of the letter from the local post office, stating the software was not shipped in sufficient protective packaging to ensure the CD wasn't damaged during shipment.

A copy of my letter sent when I returned the software package as proof that it was received in a manner in which I was unable to install the software, which would have voided the return policy conditions. (The CD was broken in half!)

A copy of the receipt showing the package return postage cost.

A copy of the dated and signed receipt indicating that your company received the package.

Please see that my replacement software is shipped immediately. If I do not receive it within ten business days from this date, I will expect a full refund for my purchase, plus the return shipping costs.

Sincerely,

Adam Dotcom

Enc.

If you don't receive a satisfactory response, consider filing a complaint with your local Better Business Bureau and sending them a "cc" of subsequent correspondence. Keep in mind that it's common courtesy to allow a business sufficient time to rectify your complaint before you threaten them.

Congratulatory Notes

One of the nicest "gifts" you can give someone is an acknowledgment for a job well done or other achievement. There are lots of great reasons to send a letter of congratulations:

- Adoption or birth of a child
- Anniversary (marriage, business, or other special event)
- Award
- Engagement
- Graduation
- New home
- New job
- Retirement
- Special achievement (honor roll, college acceptance, publication of a book, and so on)

Congratulatory letters should be short and sweet. They should include the word "congratulations" and an acknowledgment of the accomplishment.

Never include extra news of your own in a congratulatory letter—it will look like you're stealing the spotlight.

Condolence and Sympathy Letters

According to Merriam-Webster's Collegiate Dictionary, *www.m-w.com*, condolence is sympathy with another in sorrow or an expression of sympathy. These letters aren't easy to write. (That's why so many people take the "easy way out" and send a sympathy card.) Although most people automatically think of sending a sympathy card or letter in the unfortunate event of a death, these letters can be used to express empathy for any other hardship that affects the life of someone you care about.

- An accident or injury
- A devastating natural disaster
- A financial loss, including a job loss or bankruptcy
- A divorce
- A miscarriage or stillbirth
- A serious illness or injury
- A violent crime

When writing a condolence letter, it's appropriate to include the following things:

- The victim's name.
- An explanation of how you learned of the news.
- A brief, appropriate expression of your feelings of loss or grief.
- An offer of thoughts or prayers in keeping with your faith, stated in a way that doesn't offend the beliefs of the letter recipient.
- A sentiment offering affection, comfort, or hope for the future.
- A specific suggestion about how you'd like to offer assistance.

At the time your letter is received, the recipients are grieving, so you shouldn't be trying to cheer them up. A condolence or sympathy letter is simply an acknowledgment of grief that reflects the compassion you feel. Don't belabor your point: Phrases like "he's in a better place" or "God's will" can be insulting, not comforting.

Whenever possible, a short sympathy note for a friend or family member should be handwritten on plain, personal stationery. A card is also appropriate if you include a handwritten sentiment as well. Longer messages, or those sent to a business acquaintance, may be typed.

Sample Condolence Letters

Death

(Date)

Dear Becky,

I was sorry to hear about the death of your brother. While growing up, I remember how envious I was of your having an older brother. Matthew was always so considerate whenever I visited your house. I never once remember hearing him complain when he had to help us fix one of our bikes or later, when we were older, drop us off somewhere if he was going to be using the car. It's a sad fact of life that living so far away has meant that I've lost touch with some of those peripherally close to my life. I'm glad that we've remained friends, even at such a long distance—and I want to let you know that even though I'm not physically there to help, I am here for you in your time of loss.

With love,

Sue

Natural Disaster

(Date)

Dear Cheryl,

I just learned about the fire. Thank goodness everybody in the family is safe! Still, our hearts go out to you in what has to be a difficult time. I know how much pride you take in your home, and grieve knowing you've not only lost possessions, but treasured and sentimental keepsakes as well.

Larry and I are planning a trip to visit his parents next weekend, so I'll give you a call later this week to inquire about what you need—and about how we can help.

You remain in our hearts and prayers. Hang in there!

Warmly,

Sarah

Victim of Crime

(Date)

Dear Chris and Jeremy,

Powell and I just heard about the vandalism done to your place. Any invasion of your home is not only frustrating, it invades your sense of safety, too. Your home should be your haven and if there's anything we can do to help restore some semblance of order to the chaos created by this crime, you only need to ask. In fact, I'll make it easy for you to ask by giving you a call before the weekend to see when and how you can use our help.

Sincerely,

Baxter

Death of a Pet

(Date)

Dear Mildred,

Please accept my condolences on the death of your beloved Shadow. I know she was more than a cat; she was a part of your family. There's seldom a day that goes by that we don't talk, but sometimes such familiarity can lead to the assumption that things are understood. I didn't want to take that chance. This note is to let you know that I care.

Warmest wishes,

Gertrude

Loss of a Baby

(Date)

Dear Gloria and Benjamin,

John and I were saddened to hear that you lost the baby. We know how much you both were looking forward to having another child. Please know that we're here to help in whatever way we can during your grieving process.

With love,

Judy

Serious Illness or Injury

(Date)

Dear Jennifer and Mark,

David and I were devastated to learn about Jeremy's illness. As parents, we do all within our power to protect our children. For those times when life throws something in our paths that we're powerless to help a child avoid, all we can do is pull together—and find the strength to endure. Please know that all of you are in our thoughts and prayers.

Warm regards,

Janet

Terminal Illness

(Date)

Dear Joshua,

I hope you don't mind, but Jason told me about your illness. Please know that you are in my heart and prayers. I'll give you a call soon. I'm hoping you'll feel up to having me drop by for a visit soon.

Also know that if, at any time when I call, you don't feel up to talking, you should tell me so. I won't be offended. I'll understand. I only want what's best for you.

I'm looking forward to seeing you as soon as you're up to it.

Fondly,

Janet

A terminal illness doesn't mean that the victim's death is imminent. Treatments for cancer and AIDS now offer patients extended hope for the future. Despite relapses and crisis moments, chances are the patient will continue to enjoy life for years to come. Keep that in mind when you write your message.

Get-Well Letters

Whether you're sending a get-well card or writing on stationery, your message should be optimistic and cheerful, and offer assistance if appropriate.

Acknowledge the reason for your message without being dramatic. "Your fall on the ice" is more sincere than "that unfortunate accident."

Sample Get-Well Note

(Date)

Dear Bert,

I was sorry to learn that you sprained your back when you fell on the ice. I'm writing this note to let you know that you're in my thoughts while you recover, and to let you know that you don't need to fret about keeping your walks and driveway cleared. Until you feel up to doing the work yourself again, I'll gladly bring my snow blower next door. I'll see that my son Dennis follows along behind me with the snow shovel. (Miraculously, I've managed to convince him that when he shovels snow, he's building those biceps that so impress the girls.) I'll give you a call in a few days to see if there's any other way I can help out. After all, what are neighbors for?

Rest up and you'll feel better before you know it!

Sincerely,

Andrew

Invitations

Wedding and graduation invitations are traditionally formal, engraved announcements. However, those aren't the only occasions for which you'll want to extend invitations. Other occasions, such as business, civic, or cultural events and parties; educational programs and conferences; and family celebrations, like graduations, baptisms, or bar mitzvahs, might also warrant invitations.

The nature of the event will set the tone for the type of invitation that's appropriate. Formal occasions require a more formal invitation. You can be more flexible when inviting people to attend an informal event.

It's essential that an invitation contain all of the who, what, where, when, and why information. In addition, the how information is often "how much." (If there is a fee for attending the event, you need to state so somehow up front.) Order all of this information logically.

Information about attire should go on the lower right-hand corner of a formal invitation. Attire descriptions include black tie, casual, costume, evening attire, formal, informal, semi-formal, and white tie.

Sample Invitations

Formal Invitation

The Mercer County Art League
Invites you to attend
The Twenty-Fifth Annual
Local Artist Recognition Open House
to be held at
The Grand Lake Lighthouse Pavilion Banquet Room
on Sunday, the twenty-seventh of April
Two thousand and five
One o'clock to five o'clock

Refreshments   Informal Dress
Open Bar

Informal Invitation

(date)

Dear Alex and Amanda and family,

Summer's almost over so it's time to make plans for our Annual Neighborhood Labor Day Weekend Cookout. (Where has the time gone?)

We'll be holding the cookout on Sunday, September 5. As usual, we plan on eating at about 3 P.M.—and throughout the rest of the evening, as long as the food holds out.

As in the past, we're hoping you'll bring a side dish and a dessert to share. Dennis will be up at the crack of dawn, smoking ribs and getting all of his other specialties ready for the grill. We'll provide the:

> *Buns*
> *Paper plates*
> *Napkins*
> *Silverware*
> *Meat*
> *Condiments*
> *Beverages*

However, feel free to bring along any extra soft drinks, heartier beverages, or other things you wish to share as well. (Your homemade bread and butter pickles were a hit at last year's event!)

You know where to reach us if you have any questions.
Hope to see you there!

Sincerely,

Dennis and Ann

Announcements

An announcement is a formal or informal notification of an event, stated in the fewest possible words. An announcement should include the important who, what, when, where, and why details. The reasons for sending announcements are many, including:

- Adoption
- Address change
- Birth
- Death
- Divorce
- Engagement
- Graduation
- Job change
- Meeting
- Name change
- Promotion
- Retirement
- Wedding

Sample Announcements

Impersonal (sent to business associates)

Following the divorce, the former Rebecca (Becky) Millford adopted her maiden name and is now known as Rebecca Brown. She continues to reside at 2345 Homestead Lane, Smalltown, OH 45822, (419) 555-5555.

Personal (handwritten notes to friends and relatives)

Because of my divorce, I've decided to go back to my maiden name. So, from now on, I'll be known again as Rebecca (Becky) Brown. I still reside at 2345 Homestead Lane, Smalltown, OH 45822, (419) 555-5555.

Thank-You Notes

As a general rule, thank-you notes are flexible when it comes to the beginning, middle, and ending format. Regardless of the style you adapt, make sure to give enough detail and explanation when you acknowledge the gift or event, and end with a sentiment that leaves a lasting impression.

There's no specific rule about how to thank someone for a cash gift or a check. However, rather than specifying the amount, it's often more tactful to write, "thank you for your generous gift of cash" or "your check."

Sample Thank-You Notes

Note Accompanying a Thank-You Gift

(Date)

Dear Mr. Jones:

On behalf of the Wheat Fields Public School PTA and myself, please accept this framed photograph of you presenting your generous check to our organization as our sincere way of saying thank you for all that you've done to help support our school.

Because of your financial assistance, we were able to meet our goal. This summer's Reading is FUNdamental Program will be possible because of your help. Throughout the summer, we'll keep you posted about how the program is progressing. In fact, should you be able to find time in your busy schedule, we're hoping you might like to attend one of the sessions.

Thank you again for your thoughtful gift.

Sincerely,

Anthony Rice
Secretary

Gift Thank-You Note

(Date)

Dear Uncle Norman and Aunt Beth,

I just received your generous gift of a Palm Pilot. Your gift will help me keep track of all my commitments at college. I'm already entering items in the address book, so I'm well on my way to getting organized. Your gift suited my needs perfectly.

Your nephew,
Archie

Check Thank-You Note

(Date)

Dear Grandpa Jones,

Thank you so much for your generous check. I deposited most of it in my college tuition fund; however, I did keep out enough to buy a backpack. (I wanted to get something to remind me of you every time I go to class.)

With love,
Amber

✍ Typed Thank-You Notes?

Handwritten thank-you notes are usually best, but if your handwriting leaves something to be desired—or a condition like carpal tunnel syndrome makes writing difficult—it's fine to use a handwriting font on the computer.

Wedding Gift Thank-You Note

(Date)

Dear Aunt Anna,

Thank you for the beautiful hand-embroidered pillowcases. We're using them in the guest bedroom. They look lovely! Knowing how much time and love went into making them makes them even more special.

Love,

Randy and Lara

Thank-You Note for Hospitality

(Date)

Dear Dennis and Ann,

Thank you for the invitation to spend the weekend with you at your vacation condo. Rick and I had a wonderful time.

Sincerely,

Tam

Thank-You Note for Service

(Date)

Dear Pat and Homer,

Thank you so much for volunteering to let the kids spend the night. Your thoughtfulness meant that I was able to get to the hospital early enough for mom's surgery without needing to get the kids out of bed and take them to the sitter's. They always have such a good time at your house, so they were thankful for the chance to have an extended visit, too.

Warmly,
Connie

✍ Break Out the Adjectives

A thank-you note is one place where extra adjectives are acceptable. Just keep in mind that your language needs to sound sincere, not overly dramatized. The amount of flowery language you use is determined by how familiar you are with the person to whom you're addressing your letter.

E-mail Correspondence

As a result of recent technology, correspondence has undergone some changes in the electronic age. E-mail is a fast, convenient, and easy method of communication, but like all other forms of writing, there are certain considerations to bear in mind. Because e-mail is such a high-speed form of communication, people often don't consider the ramifications of what they're sending. Messages can be interpreted differently, and some unintentional meanings can arise. You have to be particularly careful that your message won't be taken the wrong way once it's received.

E-mail Etiquette

Business e-mails should be concise and to the point. People in the business world receive many e-mails per day, and the amount of time it takes to wade through these e-mails puts a severe dent in the workday. The language used in a business e-mail shouldn't be overly colloquial. Remember, a certain level of decorum is expected in any business communication.

With personal e-mails, you have some flexibility in your approach. While you don't have to be as strict in your approach as you might be with business correspondence, an upset friend can be just as bad as an upset business colleague, so you should still try to be careful with the language you use.

Whether business or personal, it's considered bad form to dash off a one- or two-word response, such as "I agree," or "okay," to a lengthy e-mail. Take a minute to summarize the point to which you're responding. This is common courtesy, and it makes the other person feel as if you're giving him or her due attention.

Key E-mail Elements

There are a few specific elements that are essential to a useful e-mail:

- A specific subject line: Many people are bombarded with so many e-mails every day, they must quickly decide which e-mails need an immediate response, and which can be left for a later time. Make sure your e-mails include a descriptive subject line. Otherwise, you risk having your message pushed back or ignored.
- An appropriate salutation: In the business world, use a regular salutation line, such as Dear Fred, or Dear Mr. Brown. In a personal setting, you can use something more colloquial, such as, "Hi, Bethany!"
- Detailed signature lines: For business purposes, it's a good idea to include information about yourself, such as your name, job title, and contact information, at the end of your e-mail. Almost all e-mail programs allow users to specify a few lines that will be attached at the end of every e-mail sent.

Forwarding E-mails

Although it's easy to click the forward button and send a message you've received to others, be considerate of other people's busy schedules. Before you forward the e-mail, do the following things:

- Delete the past e-mail addresses from the text of the e-mail, so new readers aren't annoyed by the laundry list of people they must scroll through to get to the actual information.
- Edit the subject line. Many e-mail programs insert a "fwd:" comment at the beginning of the subject line. If a message is forwarded many times, these comments quickly fill up the line. One "fwd" comment is sufficient.
- Use the "blind cc" option if you're sending a message to a great deal of people, to suppress the listing of tons of e-mail addresses that aren't necessary for everyone to see.

Recently, e-mail viruses have caused companies to re-evaluate how they accept messages from outside sources. Some have gone to the trouble of denying all attachments, stripping away the attached files at the server before it hits the recipient's inbox, or deleting the e-mail altogether without delivering it. Therefore, it's always a good idea to obtain permission to send an attachment before you send it.

Chapter 4

Doing Your Research

L etter writing is something you need to know how to do to get by in everyday situations. But what about when it comes time to write more in-depth, complicated pieces? Choosing a topic to write about is only the start. Before you can analyze your topic, you need to know how to research effectively.

In much the same way that you hone the focus of your subject matter, you also must customize your research quests—whether it's while looking through resources at the library, posing questions to experts, or conducting searches online. Focus is what lets you narrow a broad topic down to something manageable. This chapter will give you the quick tips you need to do focused, productive research, including finding the right information, making good use of library and Internet tools, and citing and documenting sources.

Types of Sources

Any research that you do will involve using two types of sources:

1. **Primary:** Published and unpublished materials that can include (but aren't limited to) public records (birth certificates, deeds),

research notes, first-hand anecdotal observations (oral history or personal diaries), and so forth.

2. **Secondary:** Published works such as almanacs, books, directories, encyclopedias, and so forth.

Secondary sources are the easiest to track down, which makes them less of a cost investment in terms of both money and time. Because of their ready availability, these materials are most helpful during your preliminary project-planning stage, when you need to read general information to gain an overall grasp of the subject. General information helps you to zero in on the specialized direction your project can take. It shows you what is already known about your topic, what aspects have been covered by others and in what ways, as well as what additional details you'll need to ascertain before you can truly establish your focus.

Library Research

Libraries are the best means for locating secondary sources. Many libraries now have their catalogs online, so you can see which books are available on the shelves and through interlibrary loan. More and more of the information that was once only available in reference books is now making its way into online archives. Often, the best information is only available through expensive subscription databases, but many libraries let you access those services through their Web sites.

✍ Straight from the Source's Mouth

One good way to gather primary source material is to go directly to the source and interview someone. Whether you need anecdotal information or verification of facts from an expert, you'll benefit greatly.

The types of resources available to you on-site will depend on the type of library you use: an academic library at a large university, a public library in a large (or small) community, a high school library, or a specialized library.

Printed materials available at the library include:

- Directories
- Nonfiction books (including textbooks and reference books)
- Newspapers
- Periodicals (popular, trade, and scholarly magazines and journals)

You can access the following databases through many libraries (you can also use them on your home computer, through a paid subscription):

- **Biographies Plus Illustrated:** H. W. Wilson's collection of more than 120,000 biographies from more than fifty reference titles, thousands of biographical magazine articles, and more than 32,000 printable images. You can search by name, profession, ethnic background, place of birth, and more. Literary criticism articles are also accessible.
- **SIRS Discoverer:** Interactive reference database that consists of full-text articles constructed from more than 1,600 magazines, newspapers, and U.S. government documents. This online resource is geared for the younger (1–9 grade reading level) researcher.
- **EBSCOhost Databases:** Access to the Academic Search Premier, Alt Health Watch, Business Source Premier, Computer Source: Consumer Edition, Eric, Health Source: Consumer Edition, Health Source: Nursing & Academic, MAS FullTEXT Ultra, MasterFILE Premier, MEDLINE, Middle Search Plus, Newspaper Source, Primary Search, Professional Development Collection, Psychology & Behavioral Science Collection, Religion & Philosophy Collection, Sociological Collection, and Vocational Search & Career Collection databases, plus:
    - **Newspaper Source:** Full text of 245 regional U.S. and eighteen international newspapers, six newswires, and indexing and abstracting of four major national newspapers, and other options.

- **Primary Search (library.boisestate.edu/reference/help/ primarysearch.htm):** Another database primarily geared to children, this one includes *Encyclopedia of Animals*; *World Almanac for Kids*; *Funk and Wagnall's New Encyclopedia*; a compilation of essential documents in American history; and collections of pictures, maps, and flags.
- **Middle Search Plus:** A daily updated database for older elementary students that includes Primary Search and adds full-text articles from more than 140 middle-school magazines, full text of fifty-two reference books, and more than 5,000 book reviews, with full-text backfiles dating to 1990.
- **Educational Researcher:** Full-text articles and graphics from more than 1,500 domestic and international newspapers, magazines, journals, and U.S. government publications, plus access to additional content that includes Today's News, Maps of the World, World Almanac excerpts, Spotlight of the Month, Issues in Government, Directory of Publications, and other constantly updated topics.
- **Electric Library:** A full-text database filled with:
  - Hundreds of popular magazines and scholarly journals such as *Consumer's Digest* and the *Journal of the National Cancer Institute*.
  - Hundreds of reference and historical sources such as the Colliers Encyclopedia CD-ROM and the *World Almanac and Book of Facts*.
  - Thousands of television and radio transcripts.
  - Thousands of photographs and maps.
  - Dozens of current newspapers and newswires such as *USA Today*.
  - Dozens of children's publications.
  - Classic books.
- **Encyclopædia Britannica Online:** Includes all of the text of the print set, plus thousands of additional articles, digital images, Internet links tied directly to the articles, statistics for more

than 190 nations, Merriam-Webster's 10th Collegiate Dictionary (including pronunciation guides and word histories), and special multimedia databases.

- **netLibrary:** Access to any of the 2,800 eBook (full-text electronic versions of published books) titles in the OPLIN collection from academic, corporate, public, and school libraries.
- **NoveList:** A 120,000-title database, searchable by subject or 350 genre categories, including science fiction, romance, mystery, fantasy, horror, western, and adventure.
- **TOPICsearch from EBSCO:** Full text for over 50,000 articles from more than 3,000 sources that include international and regional newspapers, covering such topics as aging, arts, communication, computers, consumerism, crime, current events, drugs, education, energy, environment, ethics, family, food, health, human rights, mental health, money, multiculturalism, people, religion, sexuality, sports, transportation, women, work, and world affairs.

🖾 *Evaluate Your Sources*

Always check the copyright date of any book you intend to use for research. While this information won't be as critical in a book about the Civil War, it can make a difference if you need to write about something more current. A book about breast cancer treatments published in 1990 may still include useful information, but you can't rely on it for details on treatments currently in use.

Because most libraries also now post the e-mail addresses for reference librarians on their Web sites, you still have the ability to ask questions when you're accessing the library from your home computer.

Internet Research

There's a vast amount of information available online, which is a mixed blessing. Chances are, if you know how, you'll be able to find the information you need. But when you don't know how to "refine" your search, locating information can be a daunting task. All those pesky popup ads and other distractions you encounter are definite disadvantages of conducting your research directly on the World Wide Web. You also can't always trust the information you find: As *www.snopes.com* and other Urban Legends sites will attest, tall tales abound on the Web. Despite those problems, as long as you keep your online searches focused, the World Wide Web does have advantages. For example, you can:

- Do a keyword search at online bookseller sites (*www.amazon.com*, *www.bamm.com*, *www.bn.com*, and others) to see what books are in print or about to be published in your topic area.
- Do a Web search. The potential sources of information available through this route are endless. You can check Web sites to find organizations or associations, anecdotal information on personal Web sites, newsgroups, and mailing lists.
- Read recent news articles. You can find current editions of newspapers—both large (*www.nytimes.com*, *www.washingtonpost.com*) and small (*www.dailystandard.com*)—online. (Many newspaper sites do charge for all but the most recent articles in their archives; however, you can often access older articles through a library subscription database.) For medical news, search Web sites like WebMD (*www.webmd.com*) or in the latest headlines at sites like Yahoo!'s News and Media (*http://dir.yahoo.com/News_and _Media*).

Search Syntax

You'll save yourself time and frustration wading through nonessential information if you learn a few simple rules about how to speak the language, or "search syntax."

Search syntax is the set of rules that lets you refine a Web search and retrieve only the information that is most relevant to your needs. It allows for searches based on combinations of terms, exclusion of nonessential terms, multiple forms of a word, synonyms, and phrases.

✒ Organizing Your Research

As you research, you'll need to take notes and keep them organized, whether on your computer or on note cards. Don't rely on memory. Recording your sources carefully, in bibliographic format from the start, will save you from backtracking to find information later. Also organize your materials in logical groups. Inadvertent gaps in your research will stand out, and you'll know where you still need to find resources. The more organized your research, the easier it will be to see when you're ready to begin writing.

Wildcards and Truncation

This syntax allows a symbol in the middle of a word (wildcard) or at the end of the word (truncation). This feature makes it easier to search for related word groups, like "man" and "men" by using a wildcard such as "m*n." Truncation can be useful to search for a group of similar words like "invest, investor, investors, investing, investment, investments" by submitting "invest*" rather than typing in all those terms separated by ORs. This search would also yield pages that include "investigate, investigated, investigator, investigation, investigating." To solve this problem, combine your wildcard search with related terms and the appropriate Boolean logic operators:

invest* AND stock* OR bond* OR financ* OR money

Boolean Logic

Use AND, OR, and NOT to search for items containing both terms, either term, or a term only if not accompanied by another term. Be sure to check the instructions for the search engine you're using. In most cases, "and" is assumed, so it isn't necessary to type it; separating your search words by spacing is sufficient. Also, some search engines now offer advanced search pages. The logic on those pages is the same, but rather than use the Boolean operators, you place your search words in the appropriate spaces on the search form.

Capitalization

Use capitalization when searching for proper names. For example, a search on "Herb" would exclude most instances of garden or culinary herb, yet give you those pages with the name Herb. It can also be used if you want to look for a particular pattern of capitalization, like WebMD.

Field Searching

Database records are separated into fields, which can help if you recall the domain on which you found what you needed but only remember certain key words from a title. For example, searching for these key words: "silk shirt blueroses.com" results in showing you the Web page for My First Silk Shirt on that domain.

Phrase Searching

This search is useful when you know what you're looking for involves specific words that always appear next to one another, such as in a quote. On most search engines, the phrase itself should be enclosed in quotation marks: "a rose by any other name."

Proximity

Also known as a NEAR search, some search engines (like *www. altavista.com*) let you search for terms that appear near one another, within so many words or paragraphs, or adjacent to each other.

Citing Sources

The primary citation elements of a bibliographic reference are typically the same for most styles of documentation. Primary citation elements include the name of the author; the title of the work; the place of publication; the publisher's name; the date of publication; and a page number of the reference. Many styles also include a category for the publication class or type.

Electronic sources don't always contain all of those elements and sometimes include other elements specific to this new area of publishing. Some of these include:

- Login name, nick (online nickname), or alias instead of an author's name.
- File name instead of a title.
- Protocol and address (such as a URL) instead of the place of publication and the name of the publisher.

With Web references, the need for pagination and an index becomes redundant, because any word or phrase within the text can be located via the "Find" command. Therefore, while published works usually show navigational references such as page, section, or paragraph numbers at the conclusion of the citation (and separated by commas), most online works citations omit those entirely.

Regardless of the differences in how you cite a work, you still must cite it somehow. According to the *Columbia Guide to Online Style* (*www.columbia.edu/cu/cup/*): "When in doubt, it is better to give too much information than too little."

Citing Sources Within Text

Parentheses are used to set off citations that appear within the text of a document. There are two primary types of in-text citations. The formats are as follows:

- **Humanities style:** for print publications, author's last name and page number of reference; for online publications, author or file name
- **Scientific style:** for print publications, author's last name, date of publication, and page number; for online sources, date of publication, or date of access if no publication date is available

---

✍ One Book Leads to Another

Once you find a reliable book that's informative about your topic, check out the bibliography. Chances are, those books the author found most helpful will benefit your research, too.

For scientific-style Web page citations that don't indicate a publication date or date of last revision or modification, the citation should show the date of access instead, in day-month-year format: (30 Aug. 2002).

Bibliographic Citations

Bibliographic citations generally follow MLA or Chicago for humanities style or APA or CBE for scientific style. When citing online sources, you can modify these basic formats accordingly:

- **Humanities Style:** Author's last name, first name. "Title of document." Title of complete work [if applicable]. Version or file number [if applicable]. Document date or date of last revision [if different from access date]. Protocol and address, access path, or directories (date of access).

> Ehlers, Eric. **"An Online History of the Literature of Comics."** Comics History. 2002. **http://www.thelemur.net/comics. html** (28 Aug. 2002).

- **Scientific Style:** Author's last name, initial(s). (Date of document [if different from date accessed]). Title of document. Title of complete work [if applicable]. Version or file number [if applicable]. (Edition or revision [if applicable]). Protocol and address, access path, or directories (date of access).

> Ehlers, Eric. (2002). *An online history of the literature of comics. Comics history.* **http://www.thelemur.net/comics.html** (28 Aug. 2002).

✍ *When to Repeat the Author's Name*

In a print source citation it's acceptable to omit the author's name in subsequent references to the same work (give only the page number or location). When citing an online source, however, repeating the author's name may be the only way to acknowledge where the information originated.

Here are just a few of the Web sites that can help you find materials to help you in your research:

- **AltaVista** (*www.altavista.com*): This search engine and directory includes the Boolean logic operator NEAR, which finds documents that include designated words when they appear within ten words of one another.
- **bizjournals.com** (*www.bizjournals.com*): A site for city business journals.
- **American Demographics** (*www.demographics.com*) **and Fast Company** (*www.fastcompany.com*): Business-related sites.
- **U.S. Department of Commerce Market Access and Compliance** (*www.mac.doc.gov*): Free market data.
- **U.S. International Trade Administration** (*www.ita.gov*): Market statistics.
- **U.S. Securities and Exchange Commission** (*www.sec.gov*): Public company filing information available for download.
- **Library of Congress** (*www.loc.gov*): This is the largest library in the world, with 18 million books, 2.5 million recordings, 12 million photographs, 4.5 million maps, and 54 million manuscripts.
- **Open Directory Project** (*www.dmoz.org*): The largest directory edited by humans on the Web with (as of May 2004) 4 million-plus sites maintained by more than 63,000 editors in over 590,000 categories.

Six Steps to Productive Research

No writers want to feel as if they are spinning their wheels, getting nowhere in the research department. Follow these six steps to be sure that your research efforts are efficient and accurate:

1. Crosscheck all information and refer to original sources to verify facts if you find inconsistencies.
2. Whenever possible, consult the original source—this will often involve questioning an expert.

3. Use the telephone as a research tool when you want suggestions, encounter a roadblock in your research, need an answer to a specific question, or can't locate a person or business.

4. Consult bibliographies to find books and articles written by experts—and don't overlook the names of people quoted in your research material.

5. When you finish interviewing one expert, ask for referrals to anyone else you should speak with about the subject.

6. Keep things fresh and check the publication dates on the materials you use. If you have any doubt about whether or not there may be new findings since that time, contact the author and ask.

Remember, your reputation can hinge on the reliability and accuracy of the information you present. Even one error can cause your audience to doubt the accuracy of all of your other information. Always do thorough, conscientious research, to ensure this doesn't happen.

Chapter 5

Basic Essays

Essays are the basic building block for most types of nonfiction writing, so it's important to learn their structure and format. Once you nail those things, you'll have a better understanding of what it takes to write everything from editorials, opinion pieces, magazine articles, and newspaper features, to speeches, legal opinions, and report summaries. The principles of essay writing can also be applied to descriptive passages in fiction. This chapter will teach you the tricks of the basic-essay trade, including note taking and brainstorming, refining your topic, formulating your thesis, developing your outline, and structuring your argument.

Essay Preparation

Stream-of-consciousness writing is okay when you're jotting things in your journal (or working on essay-planning exercises), but it won't produce a polished final draft. You need a solid strategy. A contractor doesn't begin building a house before he has a blueprint from the architect. As a writer, you need to be the architect of your essay and draw up a plan as well.

Do your prep work in whatever way is comfortable for you. Some people work better with spatial cues and like to do their planning on scraps of paper or note cards that they can physically rearrange. Others prefer to do all work directly on the computer, because copying and pasting the points into the proper order is more efficient for their work habits.

✍ *Follow Your Passion*

When you're given the option of choosing your own topic for an essay, always choose one you feel passionately about. This way, the topic will hold your interest throughout the entire process, and your writing will be better as a result.

How you plan your essay will depend in part on the type you need to write. If you're writing a How I Spent My Summer Vacation–type assignment, your job is easier. You already have your topic. You analyze the question, and determine what your central issue and key supporting points will be.

If you're starting from scratch, you'll first need to determine a broad subject area, and then refine it until you isolate a specific topic or subtopic. A subject is an overall category; topics and subtopics then fall within each subject. Think of them in the following way.

Subject
    Topic
        Subtopic
        Subtopic
        Subtopic
    Topic
        Subtopic
        Subtopic
        Subtopic
    Topic
        Subtopic
        Subtopic
        Subtopic

The Topic Search

As you do your initial brainstorming to find a topic, cast a wide net. Write down everything that comes to mind, without being judgmental. Don't worry about putting your topic ideas into "fancy" phrases. You shouldn't even be concerned with how much research a topic will require or whether or not you'll need to talk with experts at this point. Just see what you can come up with.

Choose a keyword for a broad topic that interests you, then brainstorm related terms from which you can choose the focus for your essay. For example:

Topic Keyword:

Herb

Related Topics:

Culinary Herbs
Medicinal Herbs
Herb Gardens
Organically Grown Herbs
Preserving Herbs

Once you've settled on a topic idea, write down any related ideas or observations that come to mind. From this brainstorming, the central issue or theme of your essay will emerge. In other words, you'll hit on your focus. Along the way, you'll weed out some of the things you write down. Hold on to those ideas that seem like logical extensions of your central theme, then arrange them in the most reasonable order. (That order may change once you get into your research, but this will give you a starting point from which to base your outline.)

All this work will build you up to the point where you'll have the three main things you need for a well-written essay:

1. Your introduction. The essay beginning, in which you essentially give the "mission statement" for your essay, or explain what it will be about.

2. Your arguments. This is where you'll transition into the major supporting points directly related to the focus of your essay, usually devoting a paragraph to each.

3. Your conclusion. This is just what it sounds like: At this point, you'll be ready to summarize your suppositions and wrap things up.

Don't Bite Off More Than You Can Chew

When choosing the topic for your essay, it's important to consider how much time you have to complete the project. Most writing projects can end up taking longer than you expect, so it's better to err on the side of caution when you make your calculations. You'll need to budget your time for the following.

- Initial brainstorming: The process during which you choose your topic, determine the focus of your essay, and write your thesis statement.

- Research: Take into consideration the amount of time you anticipate it will take to track down your research (online searches, trips to the library, and so on) and the time you'll need to examine that research and compile your notes.

- Writing the first draft: As a rule of thumb, figure at least two hours to write each 250-word page. Therefore, if your essay assignment is for ten double-spaced pages, you'll need twenty hours to do the writing.

- Follow-up research: Budget a few hours for additional trips to the library or for other research needs that surfaced while you wrote your first draft, such as the need to make another phone call to verify information.

- Editing and rewriting: Plan on budgeting half the time it took to write your first draft—an hour per page, in other words. (At the editing stage, you can insert any missing information.)

Find Your Focus

Establish the focus of your essay as early as possible. That way, you won't spend unnecessary hours tracking down and reading research that isn't on-topic for what you need to write. Track down a recent article about the topic you're interested in, and see if the topic truly interests you. After reading the article, do you want to know more? As you read, write down questions about things that intrigue you. This will help shape the direction of your research.

✍ Where the Topics Are

Need help finding a topic? Check out www.researchpaper.com. *That site lets you search for relevant information within specific subject areas using the Electric Library (the fee for this subscription service is paid for by that Web site).*

Keep your focus in mind while you read. Is that focus broad enough to support your entire essay, yet directed enough to fit the size and scope of your project? You can be somewhat flexible at this point—you still have time to adjust the scope of your research once you've honed your focus.

Your Topic Question

Once you develop a focus for your essay, phrase that focus in the form of a question.

> **Broad Topic: Transportation in lower Manhattan**
> **Topic Question: How have the transportation needs in lower Manhattan been affected by the events of September 11, 2001?**

Such a topic question would suffice for a short paper. For a longer essay, you might want to consider broadening the topic, first giving some recent history of the transportation needs (and shortages) in that area; then describing how those needs were affected by 9/11; and finally concluding with information about how those needs are being met and what plans are under way to meet them in the future.

A topic question is important because it helps you to direct your research, identify your method of analysis, and determine your thesis statement.

Personal Experience

It's often said that writers write what they know. While it isn't necessary to write only about the things you know (read *Writing to Learn* by William Zinsser for fascinating information about this theory), you nonetheless bring personal biases based on your life experiences to anything you write. Those biases are the filters through which you strain what you encounter. Even when you approach a subject with the unbiased objective of looking at "both sides of the equation," you're still influenced by your built-in prejudices.

Prior knowledge is always a plus when you're writing, because it will take you less time to become informed about recent developments related to your topic. When appropriate, it'll also mean you can write about how your personal experience relates to the topic.

✍ *Be Ready to Brainstorm at All Times*

Keep a notepad, micro-cassette, or PDA with you so you can jot down ideas whenever they occur to you. Also, bounce ideas off of other people. Others can often provide a fresh perspective, or suggest something that hadn't yet occurred to you.

Your Thesis Statement

In a nutshell, your thesis is a brief statement of the opinion you'll be developing in your essay. In this single sentence, you'll proclaim the position you intend to take in your essay; establish the way you will organize your discussion; and point to the conclusion you will derive based on the evidence you present.

Your thesis statement becomes the main point around which you compose your essay introduction and then sets the tone for the entire essay. Keep your thesis statement in mind as you do research. Gather specific information, refine your focus, and intentionally look for critical points to help substantiate your assertions.

Your Essay Outline

One way to make planning, then writing, your essay easier is to establish a fill-in-the-blanks-style worksheet and use it to develop your outline. The following example shows a sample outline from which your essay might develop. (This example assumes the essay writer has already completed some preliminary research and is keeping the notes from that research on his or her computer.)

Essay Notes Worksheet

I. Topic Question and Thesis Statement to Be Used in Essay Introduction
Topic Question:
What's the big deal about Chronic Fatigue Syndrome when a lot of people are sleep-deprived and tired in today's busy society?
Thesis Statement:
When an illness affects more than a million people in this country, it becomes important to improve public awareness so people realize that "fatigue" means more than just being tired.

II. Essay Arguments

A. Paragraph 1:

1. Supporting Point 1
Definition of the syndrome (and the names by which it's known)
Write definition so that it includes the reasons why CFS is a significant illness, including details about the devastating lifestyle changes that accompany a diagnosis

2. Evidence (that supports the thesis statement) for Supporting Point 1:

Notes from *www.cfids.org* (word/essays/cfs/research/cfids_org.doc)

B. Paragraph 2:

1. Supporting Point 2

How fatigue is more than just being tired:

How the chronic fatigue in CFS differs from the symptom of chronic fatigue in other illnesses, such as chronic depression

Muscle weakness (How when someone with CFS walks a block, it's comparable to a healthy athlete running a marathon. Brief explanation of lactic acid release in muscles.)

Fatigue comparable to how somebody feels on chemo

Cognitive skills impairment

Headache, flu-like, and other ongoing symptoms

Related and associated illnesses (CFS patients often also cope with fibromyalgia, multiple chemical sensitivities, heightened allergic symptoms)

2. Evidence (that supports the thesis statement) for Supporting Point 2

Doctor interviews (word/essays/cfs/research/med_prof_interviews.doc)

Center for Disease Control info (word/essays/cfs/research/cdc.doc)

Anecdotal patient info (word/essays/cfs/research/cfs_patient_online.doc, word/essays/cfs/research/cfs_patient_interviews.doc)

Notes from *www.cfids.org* (word/essays/cfs/research/cfids_org.doc)

Symptoms (word/essays/cfs/research/cfs_symptoms.doc)

Related illnesses (word/essays/cfs/research/cfs_other_illnesses.doc)

C. Paragraph 3:

1. Supporting Point 3

Importance of patient, caregiver, and medical provider education

"You don't look sick"
2. Evidence (that supports the thesis statement) for Supporting Point 3
Notes from *www.cfids.org* (word/essays/cfs/research/cfids_org.doc)
Controversial or uninformed media quotes and rebuttals to those quotes (word/essays/cfs/research/cfs_controversy.doc)

III. Conclusion
As simple as it may seem, it's important for someone coping with a devastating illness to know that he or she has a support group that does not trivialize the symptoms of that illness. Such respect is necessary for the patient to maintain the self-esteem necessary.

At this stage, it's a working outline. The example above includes more things under each point than could obviously be covered in one paragraph. What's important at the time you complete your outline is to get what you know thus far down on paper. You may need to add or delete points later, depending on the overall length of the essay and the space necessary to develop each argument.

Leave enough space in the outline so that you can insert transition sentences to move from one point to the next. Also keep in mind that you'll need to reiterate your main points. The more that you can "see" taking place on your outline, the easier it will be to transform that outline into your first draft. This outline "map" will help you to impose structure around your ideas so you can avoid writing an essay that's rambling and ineffective. Eventually, your outline should stand on its own, with the ideas in a logical order. Then, as you add content around your main points, choose each word so that it supports and reinforces the logic of your outline. Ideally, your outline (and eventually your essay) should build to a point where it ends with an insightful thought in the conclusion; the evidence presented in your essay should support that insight.

As you revise your outline, arrange the evidence in chronological order or in order of importance. Writing your transition sentences will help you figure out how to best organize that evidence. It's important that it's clear in your essay why one point follows another.

Your Evidence and Reasoning

Remember, each piece of evidence—anecdotes, clarifying examples, facts, and illustrations you've gathered from your research—should support your thesis statement. In most cases, you'll want to start by giving general statements and build your arguments from there, ending with specific facts. Your evidence should be:

- Accurate
- Arranged in a logical manner
- Authoritative
- Relevant
- Straightforward, and not manipulated
- Sufficient in number to support your thesis (prove your point)

When your essay relies on reasoning, you'll want to arrange the evidence that supports your thesis in its most logical order. Some examples of how this can be done include:

- Complex to simple
- General to specific
- Highest-priority item first
- Least climactic to most climactic
- Lowest-priority item first
- Most climactic to least climactic
- Simple to complex
- Specific to general

Your Essay Argument

In an essay, your argument is how you choose to present the evidence. You can do this in a number of ways:

- A discussion: Giving both sides to a debate.
- An explanation: Describing your evidence in detail.
- An exposition: Arguing a point of view.

How you choose to present your evidence will depend on how you analyze and organize your research information, and sometimes vice versa.

When you analyze the evidence you've gathered, you break it down into its logical parts. From there, you'll be able to discern how those parts relate to each other. How you demonstrate that relationship within your essay depends on your point of view. You may choose to present information from different sources that examine unique aspects about your topic, deconstruct that information to illustrate the relationships between the different sources, and then merge them into a whole concept.

✍ Leave Things Open-Ended

Be sure your topic question is open-ended. A question that can be answered with a simple yes or no won't supply the direction you need to develop your thesis statement.

Eventually, the way in which you assemble all of your various pieces should merge to present the "big picture." Following are some of the organization patterns you can use to do this:

- Advantages and disadvantages: This pro-and-con approach describes both sides of the equation, and then draws conclusions from that evidence.
- Cause and effect: This format is most often used to describe a life-changing experience or to write about someone or something that has greatly influenced your life. You describe how you understand and appreciate the effect that other incident or person had on your development and maturity.
- Chronological: This journal-style format progresses point-by-point, with details about each point given in the order of occurrence.
- Comparison and contrast: This method compares one aspect of an object or situation with another, such as describing what it's like to live at the poverty level in the United States versus the poverty lifestyle in a third world country.

- Description: This is a point-by-point explanation of a place, person, or thing.
- Example: This is the structure of the traditional academic essay, which begins with a main argument or thesis statement, continues with at least three pieces of evidence that support the thesis, and concludes by stating what the essay has shown.
- Narrative: This method involves writing in story format and is often used in personal essays—those that describe a personal event in the writer's life and the writer's reaction to that event. By design, narratives incorporate another method as well, such as when the story is described in chronological order of events.

Tips to Streamline Essay Writing

It's important to be able to organize your thoughts quickly and write them down in essay format. Beyond writing an essay, you'll use similar skills frequently, whether you need to summarize a report or complete an essay exam. Like any skill, it improves with practice. The following tips will help you to refine your essay-writing process:

- Underline key words to emphasize important thoughts within your brainstorming notes and your research.
- Think of yourself as a reporter. As you peruse your research, write down probing questions that come to mind as you discover gaps in what you read. (This will help you know what additional research materials you need; it will also help you to formulate questions to ask experts when you interview them.)
- Use different colored highlighters to mark up your notes, distinguishing different types of facts—yellow for quotes, blue for expert names, and so on.
- Mark off material once you've used it.
- If you find yourself stuck at some point in the essay-writing process, ask yourself a question. For instance: What is the most important thing I have learned/discovered while doing research for this project?

- Summarize your main points. Write your opening and closing paragraphs first, then go back and fill in the facts necessary to support your summary.
- Simplify your transitions. If you're having difficulty knowing how to make the transition from one point to the next, start out using "the first point I'd like to make," "the next point I'd like to make," and so on; you can then revise those when you edit your draft.

These tips will help to keep you on track by focusing on the essential elements of your essay, which will ease any initial intimidation you may feel about writing your essay.

Chapter 6

Academic Writing

Once you've built a foundation for writing basic essays, it's time to tackle more complex research projects. The academic essay differs from fictional or personal writing in that it has a formal structure. In almost all instances, an academic essay must contain an argument or claim. The writer addresses an issue or a question he or she has formulated, presents appropriate evidence, and then analyzes and comments on the evidence in a logical manner. Academic essays make reference to sources and also point out illogical data, such as inconsistencies or omissions found in a source argument. Students are graded not only on their writing ability; they are also assessed on their ability to select the appropriate and relevant evidence to justify their arguments or claims.

This Chapter will take a look at the basic components and format of academic essays, followed by detailed explanations for establishing a clear thesis, outline, and ultimately, a cohesive argument. As you will see in the following sections, developing a strong introduction, body, and conclusion for longer, more complex writing is more involved than the process for writing a simple essay.

Academic Essay Essentials

Every piece of work, including academic writing, requires you to use your creativity, and most of the rules about writing for any subject also apply to academic writing. However, academic writing sometimes seems particularly tricky because most disciplines want you to use certain conventions. Like any other subject, you should read papers and books in the relevant discipline before writing your own papers. This will help you get a feel for some of the conventions and practices specific to your field.

In almost all instances, American academic essays are "thesis-driven," which means that the writer explains the main point of the essay—the thesis statement—in the beginning of the essay. As covered in Chapter 5, a thesis statement is a sentence or two that provides a summary of the position you will be arguing. It also sets up the pattern of organization you will use to present the proof that supports your argument.

In an academic essay, the beginning, middle, and end of the essay are known as the:

- Introduction: The topic statement (the what, who, and when) must be introduced; the central issue—the why and how—is also addressed. Additional comments about the aim and outline structure of the essay are also sometimes included.
- Body: This is where you analyze and evaluate the evidence you've chosen to support your thesis. (The essay argument style you've chosen will dictate the manner and order in which this analysis and evaluation are presented.)
- Conclusion: The end of the essay refers back to the introduction and explains how you met the goals of the essay. The limitations of the present work and recommendations for future action, study, or additional research are also often included with the conclusion.

Essay Format

The printed format for your essay is important. In addition to showing that you know how to follow instructions, a properly formatted essay is also easier for an instructor to read and grade. Although there are certain common formatting guidelines of which you should generally be aware, it's always important to follow the particular guidelines set forth by your professor. If you are a student, remember that your most important aid for writing is your professor. Most professors are happy to discuss questions about documentation or subject matter with students.

With that in mind, following are some basic rules to keep in mind when writing academic essays:

- Print (or type) your essay on regular white, 8½″ × 11″ paper.
- Staple the pages together (unless instructed otherwise).
- Use at least 11-point type size throughout, in a regular serif font, such as Times Roman or Courier.
- Double-space the text.
- Set up margins of at least 1″ on all four sides.
- Include a title page.

Your Choice of Voice

It's important to establish the proper "voice" for your academic papers. The voice you choose for your essay will depend on your topic. Although the hard sciences tend to be less personal in their writing, in order to achieve a greater feeling of objectivity, formal academic essays must not always be written in third person. In the humanities, writings tend to be more informal, often using the first-person and second-person pronouns I, we, and you. First person can be effective, and, unless instructed otherwise by your professor, you should use it when writing personal experience or opinion essays.

✍ Admissions Essays

If you're applying to college and need information on admissions, check out the following Web sites: National Association for College Admission Counseling, www.nacac.com; CollegeBoard.com, www.collegeboard.com; PersonalEssay.com, www.personalessay.com; and Petersons.com, www.petersons.com.

Some professors are adamant about the voice you use in your paper. If you are unfamiliar with your professor's preferences, it is a good idea to ask directly.

Your Academic Thesis

Failure to establish a clear thesis is the most common problem with academic essays. A clear thesis is essential for any academic paper—it gives your writing direction and lets the reader (often the person evaluating your work) know exactly what you plan to discuss.

Many professors demand a specific thesis sentence. Advanced writers often have a good idea of what their thesis is without relying on a single sentence to define it. But even when that specific sentence doesn't physically appear in the final paper, chances are, the writer wrote a thesis sentence before beginning the work, to remain cognizant of the paper's main theme.

Sure, the thesis is a tool for your reader, but it's also a tool for you as you write. By constantly referring back to your thesis, it will be easier for you to keep your paper on-subject and formulate a clearer, more intelligent-sounding presentation.

Often in the sciences—or even other areas, for that matter—the thesis will come from a hypothesis formed before you do your research. A hypothesis is the idea you believe will be proven (or disproven) by the experiment or research you do. Once you've done the research, your thesis might discuss whether your hypothesis was proven correct or incorrect. It should also explain any implications of your research.

A literary thesis might focus on the significance of a particular message, theme, or motif in a particular work. Any thesis must be relevant to the topics you've discussed in class, but it should also relate to a subject you are interested in. If you enjoy the subject, it will be easier to write about it.

Honing exactly what you want to say about an assigned subject can be a difficult task, but remember, a thesis can make or break a paper. Take the time to refine your idea. If your paper assignment is posed in the form of a question, you can often form your thesis by rephrasing the question as a statement. If this doesn't work, try writing down all your thoughts on the subject. Once you've laid out all your ideas, you can craft a statement that will allow you to include the highest quality ideas you wrote down.

Many papers, such as a master's or doctoral thesis, require that you get formal approval for your thesis from your advisor. Even if your paper doesn't require it, however, most professors are ready to give you their input on the subject you choose if you take the time to discuss your thesis and ideas with them.

If you are writing a formal proposal, you'll probably have to follow a certain set of guidelines. A good proposal should include your thesis statement, the approach you will take with your research, and the sources and organizational structure you intend to use. Once again, as in the case with all essays, complex research papers usually evolve over time, so don't be concerned if the end result differs from your initial proposal. Professors normally expect that proposals are fluid.

Your Academic Outline

Some people find outlines restrictive. Just remember, like the thesis statement, your outline is a tool, not a taskmaster. Academic essays must be highly organized, so it's good to have all of your ideas proceeding in a logical and related sequence. Although your thesis statement will point your paper in the right direction, it takes a well-structured outline to keep you on the right path. Plan your outline carefully, and it will serve as a map that helps you to see how your ideas progress.

When writing your outline, take the time to place your ideas in relation to each other, so you don't have to worry about accidentally repeating yourself or omitting important facts as you write. Once you get your ideas into an initial framework, you'll be able to manipulate the order in which your thoughts appear. This in turn will allow you to see the entire paper conceptually. Don't forget, your outline should be fluid. Make changes to accommodate new ideas as you go along, dropping or adding items as necessary.

Never underestimate the power of a well-organized outline: An abbreviated list of what ideas should be presented when is a handy visual tool when you start writing ten- or twenty-page papers.

Effective Outline Formats

There are two effective ways to construct an outline. In the first, the traditional format, Roman numerals (I, II, III, IV, and so on) signify main subjects. In short essays, you can use these to mark paragraphs. In longer papers, Roman numerals work better as section markers. Topics within those subjects are indented one level and defined by capital letters. As you get more specific (for example, the topic marked "C" needs more notes to help you remember where your discussion is heading), indent again and use Arabic numerals (1, 2, 3, 4, and so on). From there, you can get as detailed as you like, using lowercase letters and lowercase Roman numerals, or whatever type of alphanumeric sequence that helps you to remember your structure.

Outline for "Comics: Giving Them the Respect They Deserve"

I. Establishing Comics as Literature
    A. Function of comics
        1. communication
        2. storytelling
            a. genres
        3. aesthetic response
    B. How to read comics
II. Characterization
    A. Hero and Heroine
    B. Villain
    C. Everyman
III. Story Progression

Some people use stacks of 3″ × 5″ index cards to write out their topic notes. You can color code them with a marker or a sticker to separate main topics, then put them in the sequential order. With this method, it's easy to reorder your topic cards, which is why many people find it less confining than typing an outline on the computer.

Note cards are also convenient because you can stack them to save space on your desk or lay them out on a flat surface to see everything at once.

✍ Detailed Outlines Are for Longer Essays Only

In high school, you probably learned to write the basic "five paragraph" essay: You introduce your topic and specify three main points in the first paragraph; use the subsequent three paragraphs to discuss each topic; and restate your thesis and what you've proven in your final paragraph. You don't need a full outline for this sort of essay, because it's tantamount to writing it twice! Don't make more work for yourself in this case; simply write your thesis statement and jot down your three points.

Writing Your Research Paper

Once you've chosen a clear thesis and have constructed an outline, you're in good shape to begin writing. You need to shape your ideas into coherent sentences, flesh out those ideas that need more elaboration, and make sure you have logical transitions that carry your argument from one paragraph to the next.

In longer papers, your introduction might span longer than it would in a simple essay—maybe even an entire page. Like all writing, your introduction should have some sort of hook. Longer introductions should contain information that explains the controversy prompting your paper; they can also mention the lack of knowledge that led to your research or experimentation. Another option is to detail briefly the counter to the thesis you are about to present. Your introduction should always either contain your thesis statement or at least summarize your thesis in a way that makes it clear to any reader what the rest of your paper will discuss.

The body of your paper should discuss all the ideas you wrote down in your outline. You can decide whether you want to break your paper up into specific, self-contained sections or simply transition between paragraphs (just be sure to find out if your professor or publisher has specific preferences).

Your conclusion should be strong, and it should mention the thesis and possibly reiterate the primary arguments or idea of your paper. You'll also need to mention the implications of your discussion. The best papers point out where further discovery or observations may come in the future before bringing closure to the discussion.

✍ Present Perfect Wrap-Up

Present perfect tense is often used in the conclusion of an academic essay, to state what the writer has proven and learned from the writing experience. Phrases such as "I have been doing research that leads to the conclusion that . . ." or "experts have said . . ." are in the present perfect tense.

Polishing Your Final Paper

In the case of academic research papers—as with all writing endeavors—the first draft is never enough. Many times, as you edit your work, you'll find sections to rewrite, and there's always proofreading to do.

Always leave yourself enough time to take a break from your first draft before coming back to look at it again and finish it. Review your draft closely, making sure you chose the best words to prove your point and you stated everything clearly, in an interesting and grammatically correct manner.

As you proofread, remember that software spellcheckers and grammar checkers can't catch all mistakes. Remember either to read your paper out loud, so that phrasing errors become evident, or have a friend proofread your paper, to be sure everything makes sense. Most universities have writing centers—take advantage of those free services as well.

MLA Documentation Style

No academic writing would be complete without detailed documentation. There are many types of style for documenting sources used in academic writing, including footnotes, endnotes, internal citation, and so on. This section provides an overview of one of the most common documentation styles, the one developed by the Modern Language Association, or MLA.

MLA documentation style uses internal citation, which means when you cite a quote or an idea from an outside source, you insert parenthetical documentation immediately following the idea, including the author's name and the page number from where you pulled the information.

✍ Choosing Documentation Style

Many professors don't mind which documentation style you use, as long as it's done properly and consistently. However, always be sure to check with your professor or target publication, in case a particular style is preferred.

> **There are those who claim that comic books were destroyed by the advent of censorship from the Comics Code Authority, but others claim the Comics Code Authority actually was a long-term benefactor to the comic book industry (Nyberg, x–xi).**

At the end of an MLA formatted paper, you must include a list of all works cited. Cited works should be listed by the name of the author and the title of the article (if there is an article title), followed by the name of the publication, all separated by periods. Then the publication details follow, including (where applicable) the page numbers of the article, the city where it was published, the publishing company, and the year of publication.

> **Browne, Malcolm W. "Math Experts Say Asteroid May Hit Earth in Million Years." New York Times 25 Apr. 1996: B10.**

Magazine or serial articles may also require that you include the issue and volume number of the publication. It's extremely important to use the proper punctuation in both the internal citations and the works cited list. Also note that the first line of each work cited entry is flush left, and then all subsequent lines of the works cited entries are indented.

Obviously, print publications won't be your only source of information. Some of the works you cite in an academic paper might be from the Internet, CD-ROMs, or even broadcast media (like TV or radio). For more examples, refer to the *MLA Handbook for Writers of Research Papers* by Joseph Gibaldi. A comprehensive listing with plenty of examples, this handbook covers nearly any media or information source you might use.

For more details, you can also check the style guide published by the MLA, which is currently in its fifth edition and widely available for purchase at university bookstores.

Other Documentation Styles

If you prefer to use another style of documentation, or your professor requests that you do so, be sure you familiarize yourself with it. One good source of information on other documentation styles is *A Manual for Writers of Term Papers, Theses, and Dissertations* (Chicago Guides to Writing, Editing, and Publishing) by Kate L. Turabian.

Often simply referred to as "Turabian," this manual uses footnotes to cite works, sometimes placing the complete bibliographical information as well as occasional annotations inside the footnote. These footnotes may provide the citation information for sequential references at once.

✍ *Annotating Your Work*

Bibliographies published as books or articles without any associated paper are generally annotated, and often students are asked to annotate their own works cited lists. To annotate, you simply add a sentence or two after the publication information for a work's entry, to discuss the thoughts presented in the work and to mention how useful the work is as a whole.

Turabian also occasionally prescribes a "notes" page at the end of the main text for endnotes containing tangential but relevant information.

Unlike MLA, in Turabian style, works not directly cited in the paper may be included on the bibliography page. The Turabian format for presenting bibliographic information is also different:

> Nyberg, Amy Kiste. 1998. *Seal of Approval: The History of the Comics Code.* Jackson: University Press of Mississippi.

Most fields, including biology, chemistry, geology, linguistics, mathematics, medicine, physics, and psychology, all have preferred documentation methods. For a more complete understanding of requirements, refer to a handbook published by an organization in the appropriate field.

Bibliographies

At the end of your paper, your works cited list, or bibliography, will list all the books, articles, Web sites, interviews, and other sources you referenced or quoted throughout your paper. Start making this list before you write your outline, or maybe even before you formulate your thesis. As soon as you find a useful work, write down all the bibliographical information in the proper documentation style format. You can easily remove an unnecessary source from your list later on, but it's more of a nuisance to go back to gather information after the fact. Those extra sources will also come in handy if your paper requires you to provide a list of other related books that can be used for further research.

Footnotes and Endnotes

Footnotes and endnotes are a touchy subject. Some professors like them, while others claim MLA-style internal citation is distracting. In general, there are two reasons to use a footnote or endnote:

1. To cite a work. Footnotes and endnotes should always be used if the documentation style requires it, and never used if your documentation style asks for internal citation.

2. To provide information that, while interesting or relevant to your paper's discussion, is still tangential. These sorts of footnotes or endnotes should be kept to a minimum. If the instructor doesn't like them, they should be eliminated entirely. Most often, you can work footnote information into the main text of your argument.

With modern word-processing software, endnotes and footnotes are very easy to use. Generally, it's a matter of opening a menu and choosing whether you want a foot- or endnote. Most software will keep track of the numbering of your notes and will automatically adjust them if you delete or add a note.

Publishing Your Academic Writing

All professionals in academic circles, from quantum physicists to literary historians, have to write about their research, theories, and discoveries. It's not only part of being a student; it's also part of being an academic professional. If you want to become a professor or you plan to work in a research-related field, chances are, you'll eventually need to publish your academic writing in journals specific to your field. Academic journals may have different criteria for evaluating documentation, writing style, or format than the professor who first graded your paper. Be sure to research the proper manuscript format and comply with those guidelines to the letter.

Most academic publications have even higher standards than professors. They will require your ideas and research to be even more significant and original than student papers, and the demand for familiarity with any relevant writing in the field will be much greater. Refine your work to its peak of perfection, rewriting it several times if necessary, before submitting. You might also need to alter the content or focus of your article slightly to make it fit better within a specific journal's area of concern.

Academic writing can be a daunting challenge, especially if you are inexperienced with writing. However, the key to academic writing is organization. You don't need to be a brilliant wordsmith to write a good paper, even one deserving of publication. You just need to document correctly, establish and maintain your direction, and organize your thoughts.

Chapter 7

Writing to Get the Job Done

S trong written communication skills are integral to business, no matter what your profession. Understanding specific business-writing formats is the first step toward effective workplace communication. It goes without saying that before you can do any business writing, you need to land the job first, and that means you'll need a resume. But resumes are just one form of business writing you'll need to do. What about when it comes time to resign from a position, or when you need to write a letter of recommendation to help someone else land a job? Then there's all of the day-to-day writing at the office—requests for proposals, press packets and publicity, sales letters, announcements, and speeches, to name a few. This chapter will help you work your way through all those basics.

Writing a Resume That Stands Out

Successful resume writing is an art—you must learn the appropriate style and format, choose the right words and descriptions, and proofread carefully. Searching for a job is stressful, but you can alleviate some of that stress by crafting an effective resume. While the order of the information given may vary and additional details, such as a work summary or professional licensing information, are sometimes included, all resumes include five key elements:

1. Your name, address, phone number, and e-mail address (listed as a heading at the top of the page)
2. Your work experience
3. Your education
4. Your related activities (Note: The key word is "related." Unless these experiences highlight your work experience, omit this category.)
5. Your references

The way you organize and present this information will vary, depending on the resume format you choose.

Use Proper Format and Style

Before you write your resume, determine which format will best showcase the talents you wish to emphasize: chronological, skills, experience, or CV (curriculum vitae). Choose the format that best allows a prospective employer to see that you possess the skills needed for the job.

✍ Just the Facts

Fiction has no place in a resume, so always stick to the facts. Avoid the temptation to embellish your skills or the scope of your education. Misrepresenting your credentials can be grounds for an employer to terminate your employment.

Most professions call for resumes that are direct and to the point. Your paper should be white, twenty-four pound bond or better, and the font style shouldn't be fancy—black ink in Times New Roman, Courier New, or Bodoni. There can be exceptions, of course—if you're applying for a creative position and you're expected to showcase your creative personality, you can be more daring. That sort of job might call for colored paper or fancier fonts. Just be sure that whatever style you do use, your information is presented in an easy, quick-to-read format. When faced with a huge stack of resumes, a potential employer will only spend about twenty seconds scanning each one. Make sure yours stands out!

Remember, a resume should never have spelling mistakes, grammatical errors, or formatting inconsistencies. Always proofread carefully!

Short and Sweet

Most human resources directors say they prefer a short, concise resume. (Remember: That first "glance" at your resume is only going to last about twenty seconds.) If you have lots of experience, list the pertinent details and then summarize by highlighting one key accomplishment per position. If you have less experience, include as many important details as it takes to fill the page.

A one-page resume provides just enough information to pique the prospective employer's interest. Then, you can razzle-dazzle a prospective employer during the interview with additional details. Keep in mind, however, if you're submitting a CV or resume geared toward garnering an education-related job, two or more pages are acceptable—or even expected.

When your resume goes beyond one page, use the name line from your "letterhead" and the page number at the top of each subsequent page.

✍ Be Descriptive

Resume writing is a time to toot your own horn. Never oversimplify your previous job responsibilities or accomplishments, so show your resourcefulness. Be descriptive, and use action verbs, because they convey more impact. Impact is especially important in a resume, because you want your resume to command attention.

Sample Resumes

In a chronological resume, you start by listing your current work position and most recent education, then work your way backward. A skills or experience resume works well when you want to stress your skills and accomplishments over current or previous job titles or education.

Sample Chronological Resume

Jodi Cornelius

1234 River Road
Country Corners, PA 16727

Phone: (555) 555-5555
E-mail: jodi@isp.com

OBJECTIVE

Entry-level management position in Social Services or Human Resources

EDUCATION AND LICENSURE

2002:   MS, Human Resource Management, Ohio State University
2000:   MS, Counseling Psychology, Ohio State University
1998:   BS, Social Sciences, Ohio State University
          Licensed Professional Counselor
          Licensed Chemical Dependency Counselor

EXPERIENCE

2002–present: Shelter Coordinator
                Families in Transition—Columbus, OH
                Handle all budgetary and daily management aspects of shelter, including
                coordinating on-staff and volunteer assignments.
                Create and implement at-risk families support groups.
                Act as liaison between shelter and local funding organizations.
                Research funding grants availability and complete successful applications.

1998–2002:   Social Service Assistant
                Derrick Crisis Center—Columbus, OH
                Counseled chemical dependency victims in coping skills, providing infor-
                mation on overcoming self-destructive tendencies.
                Provided case management, budget preparation, community outreach,
                and individual and group counseling.

MEMBERSHIPS

American Psychological Association (APA)
Society of Professional Counselors (SPC)
Society of Human Resource Managers (SHRM)

References and supporting documents available on request

Level of Education

If you have a college or advanced degree, don't list your high school information. Only include high school information when it includes credentials that will help to establish your qualifications for a job. Never show middle- or grade-school data on your resume.

List Your Skills

"Skills" is another optional category often included in a chronological resume. When used, it's most often added at the end of the resume, immediately above the References line:

> SKILLS
> Draft budgets for annual corporate and government sponsorship and complete grant proposals for third-party funding sources. Oversee office, supervise and train personnel. Publish case study and other articles in professional journals, such as *Journal of American Social Service Directors and Sheltered Needs*. Possess strong mathematical and analytical skills, mastery of all Microsoft Office and other business-related programs.

Sample Skills Resume

Jodi Cornelius

1234 River Road
Country Corners, PA 16727
Phone: (555) 555-5555
E-mail: jodi@isp.com

OBJECTIVE

Position that will allow me to utilize my computer skills, with both hardware and software

RELEVANT SKILLS

Created a program for a disabled vet for a specific inventory requirement
Taught adult computer courses at a local vo-tech school
Built all computers and programmed them for a local federal prison

KEY QUALIFICATIONS

- Incorporate communication skills by writing and editing technical documentation and training manuals for local business and national publishers
- Experience using all major software
- Install, troubleshoot, and repair individual and networked computer systems

EMPLOYMENT

1988–present: **Technical Support Manager**
Computer Store, Bradford, PA
Deal with all problems with computers sold, teach basic and advanced computer usage classes, build and install computers for both personal and business use

1980–1988: **Freelance Game Tester and Programmer**

EDUCATION

Bradford Area High School, Bradford, PA, 1980
National Honor Society President, Library Club Secretary, Computer Club President

References and supporting documents available upon request

Experience Resume

Anthony Rice

1234 West East Street, Celina, Ohio 45822, (555) 555-5555, tony@isp.com

OBJECTIVE

A challenging career as a company administrator

PROJECTS AND ACTIVITIES

- Responsible for staff recruiting and interviewing
- Supervises all corporate human resources needs
- Coordinates all permanent and temporary staff
- Authorizes regulatory provisions
- Arbitrates employee disputes
- Implements market strategies
- Facilitates business and government relations

AREAS OF EXPERTISE

- Management and leadership skills
- Effective written and verbal abilities
- Proven ability to reach a targeted goal
- Strong organizational skills
- Detail-oriented and accurate
- MS Word (75 wpm)

EXPERIENCE

Office Administrator—Lenny and Mercury, Inc. Celina, Ohio, 1997–Present

Coordinate daily human resources activities, including staff recruiting, hiring, and benefits. Facilitate all staffing numbers and evaluations with company president. Conduct all personnel interviews and testing. Administer six departments. Provide for all office needs.

Assistant Office Administrator—Dennis and Ann. Montezuma, Ohio, 1990–1997

Designed and implemented efficient mailroom procedures. Coordinated word-processing team. Supported Office Administrator in executive board meetings: took minutes, distributed reports, and executed client notification procedures.

EDUCATION

Wright State University

B.A., Liberal Arts, Minor: International Relations, 1990

REFERENCES

Available upon request

✐ Salary Etiquette

Never list current or past salaries on your resume. Include such informa-
tion only when specifically asked for it, such as on a job application. But
even then, it's appropriate to list a salary range, rather than a specific
hourly, monthly, or annual rate.

Letters of Recommendation and Reference

Whether you need to write a letter of recommendation or provide a reference, or you have to request one or the other, you need to make things as
easy as possible for the letter recipient. Following are general guidelines
you should always keep in mind:

- Be direct and truthful.
- State the purpose of the letter up front.
- Provide enough details so the letter recipient can make a connec-
  tion between you and the requested or included information.
- Provide your contact information, so the letter recipient can con-
  tact you if he or she needs more details.

Checking References Letter

This type of letter can be used to request information from an applicant's former employer or named references. Such letters should include
the following:

- Applicant name and position for which he or she is under consider-
  ation.
- Information about the applicant's association with the reference.
- Specific areas about which you'd like the reference information.
- A deadline for the receipt of the requested information.
- A thank-you for the reference giver's time and consideration.

Follow-Up Letter

Writing a follow-up letter can often make the difference between accepting or completing a job or making that job the first step in the beginning of a long-term working relationship. While such letters include a "thank you" for the opportunity, they also give you a chance to refresh your client's memory about your skills and abilities. This holds true if the letter is sent to acknowledge a first sale or other first association as well. A follow-up letter helps ensure a lasting, productive association.

A follow-up letter can also be sent to inquire whether or not a potential customer or client received information you sent them.

Letters of Resignation

Whenever you need to move from one job to another, you must notify your current employer with a letter of resignation. This should include:

- The actual notification of your resignation.
- The exact ending date of your employment.
- An offer to help train a replacement, if appropriate.
- A sincere, positive statement about your employment with the company, unless you're leaving on unfriendly terms.
- Your reason for leaving (optional).

If you are in a position to provide for longer notice, then do so. Likewise, if you wish to soften the effects of leaving on "less than friendly terms" you can also offer to train your replacement. Use your judgment. Two weeks is generally accepted as the minimum notice.

Request for Proposal

While entities often submit unsolicited proposals within the organization (a suggestion for a procedural change, for example) or to another entity (to solicit business), when a proposal is specifically solicited, it is known as a Request for Proposal (RFP). This is also sometimes informally known as a "request for a bid."

Whether unsolicited or requested, a proposal is a written presentation that addresses a specific need. As a full description of a proposed plan for action, the entity (person, business, or organization) submitting a proposal should make certain it contains the following information:

- Benefits of working with the entity.
- Cost breakdowns.
- Delivery (date of completion) details.
- Performance standards details.
- Qualifications and ability to perform the actions.
- Schedule of events to be addressed.
- Time requirements.

All proposals should conclude with a summary that includes the proposal writer's recommendations.

Types of Proposals

Businesses and organizations usually deal with three types of proposals:

1. Internal: for change or proposed budget adjustments within the entity.
2. External: for change or budget recommendations outside of the entity.
3. Product: for sales or technology product or service recommendations.

The following example is written specifically for a meeting and catering RFP, but the essential elements would be the same for other RFP requests, too. If these sorts of requests are made frequently, the form should be maintained electronically (as a word-processing or other program file), so it's easy to customize.

Sample Request for Proposal

To: Director of Sales
[Business name, address, phone, and other pertinent identifying information]

From:
(Contact's) First Name:
Last Name:
Title:
Company or Organization:
Mailing Address:
City:
State/Province:
Country:
ZIP/Postal Code:
Phone:
Alternative Phone Number (cell phone or pager):
Fax:
E-mail:

Event Information:

Name of meeting or event:
Type of event (check all that apply):

❐	Business Meeting	❐	Wedding	❐	Social Meeting
❐	Bar/Bat Mitzvah	❐	Conference	❐	Reunion

Is catering required?

❐	Sit Down	❐	Buffet	❐	Reception

Preferred date: Alternative dates:
Preferred time: Alternative times:

Number of people:

Need for guest rooms or suites? Yes / No   How many?

Special considerations:
A/V setup:
Other:

Additional information:

Media Relations

Media relations are about building and maintaining awareness for your business or organization. You'll build your media list by consulting current directories and polling those within your organization to drum up suggestions for distributing your communications. Once you've established initial contact, maintaining relationships with the news media is a must.

- Keep your contacts abreast of developments: Provide a current list of section officers and issue experts, or at least a year-in-review report.
- Host an annual informal media luncheon (if appropriate), or invite individual media contacts to lunch.
- Send interim media updates by e-mail.
- Write thank-you notes to reporters after you receive good coverage.
- Familiarize yourself with the other work your media contacts do; mention and compliment them on recent stories when you speak with them, or send a congratulatory note.
- Maintain a clip, transcript, video, and audiotape file to keep track of all your media efforts.

Press Packets

The press packet (or kit) is an entity's formal, written means of introduction, used for targeted media contacts. Press packets should always be assembled for events that include the media. A two-pocket folder is generally used to hold press-packet information; the outside cover is usually embossed with the entity's logo or other identifying information. The inside of this packet should contain:

- Media liaison's business card.
- Agenda or media advisory with information about the event.
- Brochure or fact sheet about the entity.
- Press release about the upcoming event.
- Biographies of principal participants, often also containing their photos as well.

More Publicity

There are several other ways to raise awareness and spark publicity for your business, including:

- Newsletters: Newsletters are an effective way to keep others apprised of your business's or organization's developments. The length and style will be dictated by your budget and by the type of information you need to distribute. It isn't necessary, for example, to go to the expense of printing a full-color, glossy publication if your only content is a press release update without pictures.
- Trade publication articles: A meaty article in a trade publication is an effective way to ensure that a targeted audience sees your message.
- Web sites: Web presence adds another layer of credibility to an organization. Even a site that only features a company's logo and some basic information is useful. A Web site is an easy way to keep up-to-date information instantly available for those who may need or want it.

Business Announcements

Announcements are another useful way to maintain contact with customers or those in the media, and also establish new business. A loyal base of people familiar with your business helps ensure a healthier bottom line.

Announcing a New Acquisition

Announcing a new acquisition not only gets your name in front of your customers again, it is also a subtle way for your business to boast about its successes.

Sample New Acquisition Announcement

Dear Customer:

It is with pride that ABC Widgets announces our recent purchase of XYZ Industries. This acquisition of one of the nation's most respected manufacturers of sprockets will not only help ensure we have a reliable supplier for this necessary component of an efficient widget, it also adds an additional five thousand employees to the ABC Widgets family.

For the past ten years, our goal at ABC Widgets has been to manufacture and distribute the most reliable widgets in the industry. We value your ongoing business and continued faith in our company, and recognize that as proof that you have trust in our abilities to meet our objectives.

If you have any questions, please contact your sales representative.

Thank you for your continued business and support.

Sincerely,

[Name]

Announcing New Hours and Services

Your customers need to know when they can reach you and what services you provide. Don't assume this information is common knowledge. Make use of every opportunity to remind them of these essential details about your company.

✍️ Take an Offensive Stance

If you anticipate industry concerns about a recent acquisition (loss of jobs, employee relocation, etc.), address them in your acquisitions announcement letter. Taking the offensive lets you put your spin on the presentation, rather than having to defend your company against unfavorable news.

Sample Change of Service Announcement

Dear Customer:

You spoke and we listened!

As of Sunday, September 29, 2005, we're expanding our business hours:

Bethany's Bakery will now be open 24 hours a day, 7 days a week.

Bethany's Bakery will continue to be closed on Thanksgiving and Christmas; however, we're confident that our widely expanded hours will help make sure you have time to place your orders and get what you need in plenty of time before those busy holidays.

We're also expanding the information available on the Bethany's Bakery Web site. Now when you visit our pages online, you'll find news about our specials and current prices, plus pictures of our newest specialties and traditional favorites. (We challenge you to take a look at pictures of our new Chocolate Truffle Cheesecake when you visit the site and see if it doesn't make your mouth water!) We're providing this service to make it easy for you to know what's available at the shop. We can also ship most selections to anywhere in the continental United States, so you can have Bethany's Bakery send your family's traditional holiday treats to anyone who can't make it in person.

Thank you for being an important part of Bethany's Bakery's success.

Best wishes,

[Name]

Effective Sales Letters

Sales letters do more than just "sell." By including essential components of information within each letter, you alert and inform your customers. In other words, if you present your information in a way that grabs recipients' attention, it increases their desire to listen to your message and encourages them to act. The following are the most common components.

Play Up Benefits

The benefits you present in a sales letter are what convert a potential customer's "want" into a "need." Always play up benefits in your letter, and present the feature you anticipate will provide the best benefit first. Features (like size, color, and price) are important eventually, but they aren't what you're selling. You're selling the value of those features and how they will benefit the customer:

> **Features-based writing: "It only weighs . . ."**

> **Benefits-based writing: "You get the convenience of a lightweight . . ."**

Enticing Offers

An effective sales offer must present more than just special prices or services; it must motivate the letter recipient to act by conveying value and scarcity.

Every time a sales letter recipient reads your offer, he'll be subconsciously asking himself: "Why do I need this now?" Anticipate that question and phrase your offer accordingly.

> **We'll provide a hands-free headset at absolutely no cost to the first three clients who respond to this cell phone upgrade service!**

> **We'll provide a free leather carrying case to the next three clients who upgrade their service.**

✍ Phone Scripts

Preparing a phone script will help you to be more prepared on sales calls. You'll be more relaxed and confident if you know exactly what you want to say in advance. Having that information on hand will also help you be concise if you have to leave a voice mail. An effective phone script is also courteous—it helps you to keep the conversation brief, an important consideration, because everyone is so busy nowadays.

Speech Writing

Even when your audience is listening to, and not reading, your words, the basics of good writing remain the same. Depending on the purpose and occasion for a speech, there are a number of different formats you can use:

1. Word for word: The benefit of having your entire speech spelled out in front of you is that you know in advance, as you practice, exactly what you're going to say in front of your audience. There is also a disadvantage however. Especially if you're a beginner, you'll be tempted to stick to your script, so you'll keep your eyes glued to the page the entire time. Don't worry about losing your place—it won't be a problem if you adjust your formatting. Use a font that's large enough for you to see easily; double-space text; and bold transitions or key words so they'll be easy to find.

    If your speech is well-rehearsed and you're confident about what you're going to say, try one of the remaining three formats.

2. Outline: Include enough information to keep yourself on track.

3. Key words: Include the words that will be sure to trigger those ideas you need to include in your talk.

4. Graphics: Sometimes called a pictograph outline, your images will usually already be in the order you need if you're giving your speech as part of a presentation for which you're using a flip chart or overhead projector.

✍️ *Memorize Your Speech Introduction*

Never try to memorize your entire speech, without notes to fall back on. Do, however, memorize the first few sentences or your speech introduction. Knowing your opening lines helps build your confidence, and helps you to establish initial eye contact with your audience.

Chapter 8

Technical and Scientific Writing

Although good writing skills are important in any professional environment, clear, concise prose is absolutely essential for technical and scientific documents. Whether you intend to translate technical terms and instructions into more accessible language appropriate for lay readers, or you need to explain a scientific process to another scientist, there's no room for ambiguity in technical writing.

The following sections will walk you through the main parts of a technical document, the creation of a project plan, and the development of a schedule outline of key steps. You'll also learn how to identify and analyze your audience, define your project, and prepare an appropriate table of contents. And, since publisher style guidelines and templates are frequently used for this type of writing, those will be discussed as well.

The Standard Model

The standard model of technical writing style and structure has been widely used for about fifty years. This is the documentation method usually taught in schools. Most professional scientists, engineers, and other technical writers also choose to write this way. The main features of a document that follows the standard model are:

- *Abstract or summary:* A brief overview of the document, its conclusions, and recommendations if there are any. An average abstract length is about 300 words; however, some scientific journals actually specify a required length. The abstract of a scientific paper or document should be capable of standing alone to be published separately.
- *Acknowledgments:* A brief note of thanks to those people who directly helped in the document work. Although authors of novels and other less formal works often thank their friends and family, many scientists and engineers consider it slightly pretentious to do this. If the document will be published and describes work supported by a grant, the grant-awarding body may insist that it be acknowledged also.
- *Introduction:* The introduction explains what the document is about and provides context—how the work described relates to other work in the field. When describing an investigation, the introduction explicitly states what the investigators set out to find.
- *Objectives:* This optional section outlines what the documented work was expected to accomplish, why it was undertaken, and who initiated it.
- *Theory:* A description of background information needed to understand the document. For example, such a section might be used to describe a mathematical process the lay reader may not know.
- *Method or methodology or procedures:* A description of how the work was carried out, what equipment was used, and any problems that had to be overcome. For instance, if the document describes a survey, this section would explain how the subjects were selected and checked for bias, and how the results were analyzed.
- *Results:* A brief explanation, sometimes accompanied by tables and graphs. Results include enough data to show that the authors have done what they stated they would do, and that the conclusions are valid.

- *Discussion or interpretation:* This interpretation of results sometimes includes comparisons with other published findings and mentions potential shortcomings in the work. In a traditional document, the discussion section is the place where the author is allowed to be less objective than is typical in other sections. Here, it's acceptable to mention opinions and to speculate about the significance of the work. If the findings are unusual or different from other people's conclusions, writers should explain why they think this might be the case.

- *Conclusion:* The overall findings of the study. Conclusions are not just "summaries"; they are statements that can be concluded from the rest of the work.

- *Recommendations:* Here, authors give their advice to the reader. If, for example, the document is about making a business decision, the recommendation is usually what the author perceives as the appropriate course of action. The recommendations section can also include suggestions for further work.

- *References and/or bibliography:* This section allows the reader to follow up on a work. The bibliography includes the list of publications referenced during the writing of the document or in carrying out the work it describes. These publications will not usually be cited explicitly in the text. References, on the other hand, are given in support of specific assertions; they are always mentioned explicitly in the text. Normally, the citation would follow the statement the author wants to support.

- *Appendices:* Additional supporting material, such as mathematical proofs, diagrams or style examples, troubleshooting information, listings of abbreviations and technical terms, and so forth.

Documentation Plan

A doc plan, often called a project plan, is a written explanation detailing all components of a technical writing process. The main purpose of a technical document is to convey information. As such, the document should place as few hindrances as possible between the mind of the writer and the mind of the reader. Of course, if you were writing a novel, your top priority would be to entertain your reader. In a technical document, however, the information is paramount.

A good document requires careful planning. As part of the planning stage you should try to answer the following two questions:

1. What is the document about?
2. What are you trying to say?

You need to arrange things so that the key facts and conclusions are accessible. Not everyone will read the entire document, so make sure that your message is clear even if a person only skims it.

Once you understand the exact nature of your job and you know when you must complete your written documentation, you're ready to prepare your "doc plan." Begin with a "Preliminary Project Plan" to help organize information as it's gathered and considered. In order to complete your project plan, you'll need to determine the following:

- *Project description:* Think of this as the project's "mission statement"—a one- or two-sentence description of what your document should accomplish.
- *Title:* At this point, it may be a working title; as long as you have something to designate your particular project, it should suffice.
- *Project incidentals:* Notes about the purpose, scope, and limitations of the document.
- *Audience:* This is most important. Before you can proceed, you need to know who will be reading what you write, what their education level is, and how much technical expertise they have as it applies to the project.
- *The why and the what:* The reasons why the intended audience will use the documentation, and for what purpose.
- *Proposed table of contents:* Often referred to as a "fluid document," this draft table of contents is the map that details the direction your

document should take. Although you'll modify it as you go along, it helps to plot out your objective and to ensure that you're marshalling your information in the best way possible.

- *Deliverables:* Unless you're writing a technical document on assignment from a publisher, you'll often handle other details beyond just writing. "Deliverables" can include details such as whether printed copies or disk copies are to be supplied, disk and file formats (including software versions), and where and when they are to be delivered.
- *People and other resources:* Who and what resources will be available to help you? How many work-hours will be required? At what cost?
- *Change control:* This would cover procedures for relaying information about program changes to the documenter during the development of a software manual, for example.
- *Milestones:* A schedule showing appropriate milestones, such as when the documentation plan was approved; the preparation, review, and approval of each draft; the index completion; the usability testing; the camera-ready artwork preparation; and the printing, binding, and distribution.
- *Source material:* What written information is already available?
- *Standards and specifications:* Must the documentation be written to a particular standard or specification?
- *Technical edit:* Who will check the technical accuracy of the manual? Whose responsibility is it to hire (and pay) the technical editor(s)?
- *Editorial control:* Who has it?
- *Budget:* A cost estimate of how much time and out-of-pocket expense is necessary to complete the project.
- *Copyright:* Who will own the copyright and other proprietary rights? Usually, the author of a commissioned document is the first owner, unless a specific work-for-hire or other agreement states otherwise.
- *Translation responsibility:* Provisions for the translation into other languages, if applicable.

Answering these questions will help you to develop a suitable project plan. Once you have your preliminary project plan in place, you might then discuss it with your project manager. After any amendments have been added subsequent to those discussions, both parties should formally agree to the project plan.

✍ The Project Outline

Once you know the specifics for a technical writing project, you can develop a realistic schedule. This outline includes all the milestones necessary for the project's completion, including your blueprint, research, first draft, language edit (also known as the copyedit), technical edit, beta test, final review, completion of master copy, and the point when printed copies will be ready for delivery.

Who Are You Writing For?

As discussed in the beginning of this book, as a writer, you must always adapt your writing to meet the needs, interests, and backgrounds of your readers. For most technical writers, determining their audience is an especially important consideration when planning, writing, and reviewing a document.

✍ What if You're Writing for More Than One Audience?

The way you handle this will be dictated by your project, but one solution is to write each section strictly for the audience that would be interested in it, then use headings and section introductions to alert the reader to the intended audience for those areas.

Common audience categories include the following:

- *Experts:* These people know the theory or product inside and out. They usually have advanced degrees and operate in academic settings or in research and development.

- *Technicians:* These are the folks who build, operate, maintain, and repair the stuff that the experts design and theorize about. Theirs is a highly technical knowledge as well, but it's more practical in nature.
- *Executives:* These people make business, economic, administrative, legal, governmental, and political decisions regarding the things experts and technicians work on. If it's a new product, they decide whether to produce and market it. If it's a new power technology, they decide whether or not it should be implemented. Often, executives have little technical knowledge about the subject.
- *Nonspecialists:* These readers are the lay audience—they have the least technical knowledge of all. They may want to use the new product to accomplish certain tasks, for example, or they may want to understand the new power technology enough to know whether to vote for or against it in an upcoming election.

Identify your readership *before* you start work on a technical document. The level of explanation necessary for an expert audience is totally different from what is required for readers unfamiliar with your subject. For example, if you're writing for computer scientists, although you don't need to discuss what a modem is, you might need to explain what "baseband" is. When writing for people who have no knowledge of your topic, you might need to define terms within the text or include a glossary at the end.

✍️ Catering to a Range of Expertise Levels

When there's a wide range of variability in your audience, you can write for the expertise level of the majority of readers, but this sacrifices the needs of the remaining minority that would benefit from more help. To get around this, include supplemental information in appendixes or insert cross-reference suggestions to books or materials for beginners.

Regardless of the category your audience falls into, you must also consider their background; knowledge, experience, and training levels; needs and interests; and other demographic characteristics. Don't forget about their age range, area of residence, gender, political preferences, and so on.

Preparing a Table of Contents

A detailed table of contents is an integral part of any published work, but it's also a technical writer's best tool for organizing the document itself. Your proposed table of contents is the tangible expression of your vision on how the document should be organized and what it will say. It not only shows your editor or project manager that you have a strong enough grasp of the material to organize it into effective sections, it also gives him or her a chance to make sure you've covered every important aspect of the project.

Much like an initial outline, an initial table of contents is a fluid document. New information arises during the research and writing phases, which might result in sections being added to cover the new material. Your editor or project manager might also decide on a different focus for the project after viewing your initial drafts. And sometimes, additional subheads are needed to explain a point further within the document itself, rather than in an appendix.

A proposed table of contents should contain your outline of numbered chapters, parts, or sections and the heads and subheads within those parts. You'll probably need to include an estimated total page or word count as well.

Publisher Templates and Style Guides

Publishers will often have their own specific ways of putting documents together. In order to format their documents to the proper template, writers will sometimes use word-processor macros. It's simply a matter of downloading the macros, then using them when writing the assignment. Template macros are usually set to insert the necessary differences in font size and styles used for such things as chapter titles, heads, subheads, and body text. These templates save a step, because the publisher doesn't have to format the document for publication.

Many publishers that produce technical manuals also require writers to follow particular style guides, which address linguistic style as well as formatting issues. Dissimilar spelling and punctuation makes for disjointed writing, so style guides help maintain consistency. Consistency improves a writer's efficiency, lowers the cost to produce technical information, and makes it easier to maintain the project over time as different writers and editors revise it.

White Papers

A "white paper" is a document that states a position, or proposes or explains a draft specification or standard. It can be very technical or hardly technical at all, depending on its intended audience. For example, a company might have a white paper on its Web site that examines obstacles associated with a particular new technology and explains why their approach to this problem is better than other solutions. (Many Web sites for specific software products include white papers that give product specifications and usage information.)

Sometimes, white papers are articles that state an organization's philosophy or position about a political or social subject. Other times, white papers might be used to explain the conclusions resulting from a design or research collaboration, or a development effort.

Many technical writers are employed to produce white papers as supplemental sales and marketing material. For example, a white paper can be released after a new product or service is already on the market. In that case, a problem is presented and a solution (the product or service) given. Target audiences range from investors and vendors to potential customers. Often, because what you are "selling" in a white paper has already been released, it's usually safe to assume that your reader will have some background information. These sorts of white papers are distributed through many channels, including the Web, trade shows and conferences, and sales representatives.

A white paper is usually organized in three sections:

1. A summary of the problem's history.
2. Details about the solution, how it can be best employed, and why it is better than those of its competitors.
3. A summary of what is expected from the reader. This is the most important part of the paper—the "sales pitch" you've been leading up to. Make it clear and persuasive.

Next, develop an outline by expanding on each of the topics in your problem-solution treatment, using subsections and bullets that summarize the main points in each topic. Determine approximately how many paragraphs and pages each subsection will need so you can get an idea of the length. As soon as these steps are completed and approved, you're ready to start writing.

✍ Staying on Track for Nonspecialists

To make technical information more understandable for nonspecialist audiences, be sure your writing includes easily understood steps and definitions of key terms. Also, stick to the facts. Include basic instructions, examples, and graphics, but omit theoretical discussions about the topic.

Chapter 9

Grant Writing

Community interest groups and other organizations often must submit proposals for grants to access funding. When seeking grants for funding, you'll be busy writing letters of inquiry and intent to apply, completing grant application packets, writing proposals, and more. In this area, you might also encounter firms that charge a fee to find appropriate funding programs. A reputable firm may very well help you secure funding. Be careful to investigate any firm's claims, however, to make sure it isn't some fly-by-night organization that simply collects consulting fees and then disappears without a trace.

The Search for Grants

There is no rule of thumb for grant applications. Every funding program will be a little different, due to the scope of funding agencies that exist. Naturally, nothing comes free. The money you're applying for has to come from a source somewhere, and there may sometimes be strings attached. All funding programs have specific requirements that must be met in order to qualify for funding. Before you apply for any type of grant, you must first determine up front what the requirements will be.

Don't give up hope if your organization doesn't meet a particular eligibility requirement. You might be able to modify your program to make it fit those requirements.

Meeting the basic criteria will not guarantee your success, however. Wherever there's free money, there are also lots of groups clamoring to get it. You need a proposal that demonstrates your group can manage the program and achieve results as outlined in your proposal.

Strategic Assessment

In the strategic assessment stage, you will identify all of the areas you must address. Certain organizations must meet certain conditions for some types of funding, and this raises issues. For example: Will you have to include sponsorship information on your letterhead, in newspaper ads, or in radio or TV advertising? It would be terrible to have your funding pulled because you didn't comply with an advertising provision.

It's your job to know about these types of issues in advance. If you consider such things early in the proposal writing process, it will help you to avoid surprises later. Make a list, and ensure that all important points are emphasized in the proposal by including them in your strategic assessment.

Start by reviewing the criteria for the particular grant or program. Guidelines provided by the funding agency will dictate eligibility requirements. Some programs may only be open to disabled persons, or females, or people of a particular ethnic background. Before you take the time to fill out any paperwork, make sure you qualify.

You must also consider your plan of attack for securing this funding. First, determine the specific funding programs you plan to access. From that point, you can come up with a plan of attack for following the procedure through from start to finish.

Defining Your Goals

Make a wish list. Grab a piece of paper and write down everything you'd like to see accomplished. If you're working with a group, brainstorm all the ideas you can come up with. The sky's the limit on this one—just keep writing down ideas, no matter how ludicrous or bizarre they seem. This is a great way for generating ideas.

Once you're not preoccupied with worry about whether or not an idea will be okay, your mind will be free to devise some innovative ideas. Let your imagination run wild. Even if you concoct silly ideas, they can still help. Often, when you combine pieces of one "silly" idea with pieces of another "silly" idea, you cook up something great.

Concept Paper

A concept paper contains information that is similar to a preliminary proposal. You can use a concept paper to determine a project or program's feasibility; investigate opportunities that can be accessed; and identify areas that will have to be addressed to make the project work.

Although some funding agencies will require that a concept paper be submitted along with a proposal, most will not. Nevertheless, doing work on the concept paper or preliminary proposal in the early stages will make the job less tedious later. Treat a concept paper as the initial draft of your proposal, and begin it even before you've begun to investigate funding agencies. Get as much of the work done as you can beforehand. Then, you can use the information in the concept paper to draft your proposal.

✍ Budget Information

A concept paper may contain budget information, but it's usually preliminary. Ballpark figures are acceptable. Formal budgets and cash flow statements, which you will ultimately attach to your proposal, should be tailored to the program and the requirements of the funding agency. At this early stage, however, it isn't necessary to go into great detail.

Letter of Inquiry

Before you create a proposal, you may be required to submit a preliminary letter of inquiry regarding availability of funding and eligibility requirements. While it isn't necessary to go into great detail about the proposal you wish to submit, feel free to include some basic information about your organization.

Letter of Inquiry

Project title: SkaterSpace

Our organization is currently investigating ways to address the ongoing problem of teen skating activity in unauthorized areas, such as busy parking lots, parks, and malls. We believe we have a solution that will assist in reducing the amount of citations issued to teens caught skating in these unauthorized areas.

We would like to know if your agency is able to offer any financial support, and would appreciate any information regarding funding opportunities that you can provide. Yours truly,

Fred J. Esquire

Letter of Intent to Apply

This simple preliminary letter notifies an agency that a proposal will be forthcoming. Here, you should include basic information about your organization and the nature of the things you will be proposing.

If the funding agency you're approaching requires a letter of intent, it should be able to provide you with a list of the items your letter must address. If no guidance is forthcoming, it's a good idea to make sure your letter of intent includes the following:

- Name of organization
- Contact person, title
- Address
- Telephone (and extension, if applicable)
- Fax number
- E-mail address

- Web site address
- Project title
- Brief project description
- Amount requested

Your project description should be brief—no more than three or four lines. The description is only meant to make the funding agency's staff aware of the program. Your proposal will outline how you plan to achieve the goals.

A letter of intent to apply is also the place to include questions about eligibility, the application process, or any other concerns you may have. Although the actual decision makers often don't consider the letter of intent, it gives the staff and evaluators invaluable information and aids them in their case management.

Letter of Intent to Apply

Coalition for Community Involvement
Fred J. Esquire, Coordinator
123 Fake Street
Needsfunding, OH 59119
Telephone: (419) 555-9877
Fax: (419) 555-9876
FredEsq@communitycoalition.not
http://www.communitycoalition.not
Project title: SkaterSpace

Our proposal will address the current problem of teen skating activity in unauthorized areas, such as busy parking lots, parks, and malls, and will assist in reducing the amount of citations issued to teens caught skating in these unauthorized areas. The Coalition for Community Involvement has developed an approach that will benefit the community by providing a place for teens to skateboard while also removing the problem of unauthorized activity in other areas.

We anticipate that our proposal can be implemented for a cost of $5,000. We will submit a full budget and cash flow forecast along with our proposal.

The Coalition for Community Involvement is not yet a body corporate; it is a nonprofit association of interested individuals from the community. If Magma Funding requires that sponsored agencies are incorporated, we will undertake to meet your qualifications; however, we would hope that any required incorporation could be done concurrently with the execution of the proposal, so as not to delay this season's proposed program.

Should you have any questions, please don't hesitate to call. We will forward our full proposal within the next thirty days.

If you are sending your letter on letterhead, the name of your organization and its address should be obvious. If the funding agency asks for the information in a specific format, however, follow that! Don't assume that the address on the letterhead will suffice; some places are sticklers for detail, and the slightest deviance from their standard form will often result in delays.

The Grant Application Packet

Some funding agencies (particularly government agencies) provide their own forms and insist that they be used for all applications. Don't let the paperwork daunt you—it might look complicated, but it's actually your opportunity to provide all the information you can.

Answer every question on a grant application form, and fill in every space, unless it clearly says "office use only." If a particular question is not applicable, write "N/A" under the heading. This shows the evaluator that you read, understood, and answered the question. Leaving it blank might indicate that you missed the question, which makes your application incomplete.

Do not write "see attached proposal"; pull the relevant information out of the proposal and write it in on the application.

Your Proposal

Your proposal is the main source of information for the people who evaluate requests on behalf of the funding agency. Your proposal will be considered faster when you make the evaluator's job easier. If you do your homework thoroughly, an evaluator will see that your organization is capable of completing the tasks you propose.

Address every necessary point, so the evaluator won't have to do any additional research.

If the evaluator has to do a lot of detective work, it may not reflect favorably on your proposal.

Introduction

The introduction should give the evaluator a basic idea about the thrust of your proposal, touching briefly on the points raised there.

> **The Coalition for Community Involvement has been active in the community since 1975. Our volunteer members have come up with a solution to the problem of teen skateboarding and would like the Acme Funding Agency to sponsor our innovative program.**

Including too much information lessens the impact of your introduction. Save the extra details for the balance of your proposal. Some organizations now ignore the "introduction" entirely, instead submitting an "executive summary" at the beginning of the proposal.

Needs Statement

This statement identifies your organization's needs. You simply characterize the existing problem you are trying to address. Then, in your analysis, you offer solutions to that problem.

Needs Analysis

While you don't need to include a separate "needs analysis" section, somewhere in your proposal you must show how your needs will be fulfilled by the activities you put forth. A solid needs-analysis section serves two purposes.

1. By identifying how your needs will be met, it gives an indication of the dedication and thought your group has put into the project.
2. By providing the evaluator with a concrete example of how particular goals will be met, it shows the evaluator that your plan is concrete and is capable of evaluation.

Including your goals in the proposal gives the evaluator an identifiable means of evaluating the success of a particular provision. Ideally, you will achieve all of the goals you suggest in your needs analysis.

✍ Additional Information

In addition to your basic proposal, you may wish to attach additional information. You can add these as appendices, labeled either by letter or number. If you prefer, you can use "schedule" instead of "appendix." Or follow the funding agency's preferred format, if it has one.

Your Management Plan

Your management plan ties in closely with the strategy you adopt, but its elements should be considered separately. Although you should keep the following guidelines in mind, it is not necessary to include these headings in your actual proposal.

Methods

Methods dictate the means you plan to use to achieve your goals. Within your proposal, you should demonstrate the methods you will implement to ensure that your goals are accomplished.

Activities

In order for an evaluator to judge your proposal, he or she must have an idea of the activities you propose. The activities should be broken out independently, showing exactly what your group plans to do with the funding allocated to it.

Timeline and Cash Flow Forecast

The proposed timeline is one of the most important aspects of your proposal. You need to be able to tell the funding agency when certain activities will occur and when you'll require a cash influx. Your cash flow forecast—a calendar of when certain budget items must be spent—is an important complement to your timeline. You need to show the funding body when certain expenditures will be made, so that they can make arrangements to have the correct amount of cash forwarded to you before you need to spend it. To create a cash flow forecast, simply break down all of your budget items into monthly (or quarterly) cost.

Progress Reports

Once a funding agency gives you money, expect that they will want to see how it's being spent. You'll need to provide progress reports, so make sure you address this in your initial proposal. Establish which information is important, and demonstrate how you will show your sponsors that you are making progress. Success must be measurable, so define up front how you plan to measure it.

✍ Reviewing Your Final Proposal

Your proposal will appear more persuasive if you check it closely for errors. A proposal rife with misspellings and grammatical mistakes can lead an evaluator to believe that you're not attentive to detail. To enhance the professionalism of your proposal, ensure that all words are spelled correctly and that proper grammar is used. Have someone else give it a final read before you submit it.

Once this task is completed, reporting is simply a matter of filling in the blanks—just provide the information promised in the proposal. Your funding agency may have special report requirements or forms to fill out. If no forms exist, a report done in letter format is fine, as long as it includes a summary of the measurable goals you have identified.

Persuasive Grant Writing Techniques

In a sense, successful grant writing involves making sure that all your Ts have been crossed and your Is have been dotted. It's always a good idea to pay close attention to the actual language you use to identify the objectives outlined in your proposal. Make sure that your writing is positive and upbeat. And instead of using wishy-washy words like "should," "think," or "might"—use strong, definite words like "will," "believe," or "know." Here are some additional tips to consider:

- Marshall your information. Each paragraph should have only one main point. Your job will be much easier if you start with an outline; then, you can focus each paragraph of your proposal to drive home each of your points.
- Structure your argument. Developing a persuasive argument is not such a difficult task; it simply requires an organized approach. To begin, break your argument down into its basic components. This ensures that you won't miss anything along the way.
- Start with your proposition. Your proposition identifies the problem you plan to address. For your own purposes, structure it in the form of a question. While you may not use it this way in the proposal, forming it as a question in the planning stages helps you devise your analysis.
- Follow it up with facts and evidence. What information is important to address the problem you've identified in your proposition? When appropriate, include the evidence you are using to back up the facts.
- Provide a thorough analysis. Don't jump to conclusions. Even though you may understand the rationale for your argument, within the proposal you must demonstrate to evaluators that your argument reaches a logical conclusion. Demonstrate how the proposition will be addressed. Use the facts to highlight the positive effects of the implemented proposal.

- State your conclusion. At the end of your analysis, your conclusion should demonstrate how the proposition is addressed and how its needs are met. Ultimately, this is the answer to the question you formed when coming up with your proposition. The facts and analysis simply show your work and illustrate how you reached your conclusion. For example:

> Last summer, our county issued 175 citations to teenagers riding skateboards in unauthorized areas. The secondary parking area at the community college receives no traffic in the summer; in addition, it is paved and includes a number of access ramps that would be of interest to these teenagers. Allowing this area to be used by summer skateboarders would provide teens with an appropriate place to participate in their sport, while saving the general public from the inconvenience of having to beware of teenagers whizzing by on skateboards. This action may also reduce the number of infractions that occur during the season. Therefore, allowing the community college's secondary parking area to be used as a skateboarding area would benefit the community at large.

While the proposition isn't overtly stated in the passage, it can be inferred. Stated as a question, the proposition would read: "How will allowing summer skateboarders to use the community college secondary parking area benefit the community?"

Structuring your argument according to these guidelines aids the evaluator in making a decision. When you help him or her along the way by showing how the needs will be addressed, you're actually making the evaluator's job easier, which increases your chance of success.

Chapter 10

Web Writing

I n their early days, Web pages were simple because of technological limitations. Over time, Web technology has evolved dramatically, into a dynamic medium that can distribute virtually any kind of information. The advent of the Internet has prompted a new set of writing rules. Web writing raises a number of considerations, and the dissemination of this vast amount of information requires its own unique approach. Web readers expect information to be presented in much smaller segments than is common for other print-based formats. That's why in most cases, short paragraphs and clear and concise language are a must when writing for the Web.

Linear Versus Nonlinear

Whereas many other types of writing take a linear approach to development, Web writing is usually nonlinear. With linear writing, ideas are introduced gradually and are used as building blocks to form the basis of what comes later. A novel is a good example of linear writing: You have to read the beginning first, or else the middle won't make sense.

With nonlinear writing, you don't have to start at the beginning and read straight through to the end to understand everything that's presented; each section stands on its own. You should be able to start reading at any point and learn what you need to know, without having to digest the entire document.

✍ Say It Again

When writing in a multimedia format, always make sure you present infor- mation in more than one place. Never assume that your readers will start reading at the same place and follow a particular pattern. Users can browse Web sites in many different ways, so you shouldn't bury critical information.

When writing for a nonlinear purpose, each individual section must contain all of the relevant information. It might take more work to pre- pare for a nonlinear manuscript, but you'll find that once you do your prep work, the actual writing will go more easily because you'll have a compre- hensive outline. And because you'll spend extra time organizing the infor- mation, your writing is usually more concise and polished.

Increased Interaction

Reader interaction is relatively limited when dealing with printed docu- ments. Readers look at a table of contents or index, find a page number, flip to the appropriate section, and that's about it. In multimedia writing, how- ever, readers can interact with material to a greater degree and access vari- ous components any number of ways. For example, visitors may link from a site index to see only the specific page they want. The reader determines what comes next, instead of the author. This ability to choose makes mul- timedia writing incredibly dynamic.

Nowadays on the Web, people can jump from place to place by following links that connect two relevant bits of information. But it doesn't stop there. Web applications aren't just limited to the printed word. Links take visitors to relevant pictures, sound files, video files, or virtually anything else that can be displayed on a computer. The scope of applications is almost limitless.

Incorporating Multimedia Formats

Multimedia isn't a new concept. Silent movies incorporated video, sound, and text to convey meaning. In the '60s and '70s, educational filmstrips with accompanying cassette tapes incorporated similar elements for the classroom environment.

Whenever information must be conveyed, multimedia elements can be applied to make presentations more interesting or easier to understand. A multimedia presentation, including one on a Web page, can incorporate a variety of elements, including animation, music, pictures, sounds, speech, text, and video. Just remember that while an effective presentation can help users absorb your message, it can never replace relevant information.

In most cases, your emphasis will be on the information you're presenting, not the way you present it.   When designing an online presentation, decide which elements will help you to convey your information most effectively. Never use elements just because they're available. Your online presentation should only incorporate sound, for example, if it's integral to your goals.

✍ *Leave Room for Choice*

Always give users a choice to use sound or video files—never start things automatically. Not all users have fast, up-to-date computers, and extras like sound files blaring in the background can tie up resources. In fact, some people will skip a page altogether if they can't turn off background sound.

Start with the information you want to present, and then consider how to best convey it to the visitor. Remember that using sound or video technology requires expertise. If you plan to incorporate those types of elements in your presentation, but you don't know how to create the files, give yourself enough time to figure out those logistics *before* your project must be completed—or subcontract the work to someone else, if necessary.

✍ Blogs

Web logs—or "blogs"—make it easy to publish essays on the Web. You upload your work using a simple template, and then the server does the rest for you. Blogs provide an easy-to-access publishing forum that supplies visitors with current, topical information. Because they are informal, you can take whatever approach you like. Some people write full essays and upload them; others simply post short comments and observations in online journal format. You can find links to blogs online at Blogger (www.blogger.com).

Instructional Multimedia Writing

Because they display different forms of information in such dynamic ways, many multimedia projects are created for educational or introductory purposes. Typical instructional materials often include written information, audio presentations, or video presentations. Whether on the Web or in a cross-linked file, multimedia presentations can encompass all three of these elements.

No matter which formats you choose to use, your presentation should do the following.

1. Explain all concepts, terms, and other information the user will need to know.
2. Illustrate the principles and practical aspects of the information you're presenting.
3. Inform the user about new concepts, aspects, or new material.

High-Impact Online Presentations

As stated earlier, your first step when writing a multimedia presentation should be to ensure that you're providing important and relevant information. After you've identified that information, you should begin thinking about the way you'd like to convey it.

When it comes to writing for online presentations, less is generally more. Remember, you don't need to incorporate all elements, just the ones that will enhance the information you're presenting. Following are just a few of the design tools you can use to enhance the presentation of a site:

- Embedded sound files
- Embedded video files
- Flash
- Java
- JavaScript
- Shockwave

You may need to do some research to figure out how to use these tools. There are lots of online resources available to answer questions regarding Web design tools. Many sites also provide free automated Web scripts that will complete certain tasks for you. Identify what it is you want your site to do, and then set out to find the appropriate tool. If you're lucky enough to be working with a production team, hopefully you will have access to people who are experienced in using these tools.

Incorporating Text into Graphics

Rather than using simple default fonts displayed by a browser, you'll probably want some aspects of your site to appear stylized. Some Web page editors allow you to specify certain fonts, but the page will not display properly if the visitor does not have the selected font installed on his or her computer. To ensure browser compatibility, you can create graphics for headers and icons that contain the text you want to display.

You can use just about any graphic editing software to do this. However, it's important to keep a log of the following information:

- Background color
- Font point size
- Font type

- Graphic size
- Style (boldface, italic, etc.)
- Text color

You'll need this information to modify or add new headings to your site. There is nothing more frustrating than having to figure out which font or other style technique you used to re-create the look and feel of images you created months (or years) before.

✐ *Proper Color and Font Choice*

Remember that sites designed with poor color choices and font sizes can alienate some users because they create a host of problems. Not all monitors—nor all users—interpret colors in the same way. If someone is colorblind, some font colors can blend into the background color. Likewise, fonts that are too small or contain unusual design elements can be difficult for someone with vision problems to read.

Proper Online Presentation

When writing for online presentation, the first rule of thumb is to use short paragraphs, because they're easier to skim. Visitors probably won't read every word you write; they'll certainly read sections, but most will be looking for specific information. Make it easy for people to find.

Keep these additional guidelines in mind whenever you're writing material that will be displayed on a computer.

- Use proper contrast between the background and the text color. Some combinations can be impossible to read. Make your Web pages as easy to read as possible; this helps to ensure people will take the time to digest your message.
- Use a proper size font. If you use smaller fonts, make sure that your HTML code doesn't preclude users from making the text larger. You don't want to risk limiting your site's readability.

- Break up your pages. Long pages make scrolling and printing cumbersome. Split long pages into smaller sets of two or three.
- Verify your links. It is maddening for users to click on a relevant link, only to find that the page does not exist. Update your links promptly when you find out they have changed.
- Cross-index your site. Make sure you can access the index pages from any page in the site, or you may find that you lose some visitors who might land at your site via a middle page. If there is not an indication of other information available, the user may just close the window or move on to another site.

Your Web Audience

Like any other type of writing, Web writing must be suited to the needs of its audience. If you write beyond your audience's comprehension level, they won't understand your message. When that happens, users will simply click off your page and find something that's easier to understand.

Do some investigation, and try to figure out the demographics of your ideal audience. Surf the Web, and look for sites that appeal to the same kinds of users. How specific is the information they offer? Will a broad approach suffice, or will you have to break your ideas down into further specialized categories? Once you have an idea of who your visitors will be, you can tailor your approach to better suit them.

Creating Your Web Content Outline

When you put together an outline for Web content, you'll need to plan out information for the following headings. (If you're not writing for the Web, you still need to address all of these concerns; you just won't need a domain name.)

- *Domain name:* Do you want a special domain name for visitors to type in? (A Web site name like CookingWithPam.com is easier for somebody to remember than a lengthy URL.)

- *Objective:* What kinds of things do you plan to achieve with your online presentation?
- *Target audience:* Who do you anticipate will read or participate in your online presentation?
- *Resources:* What do you plan to offer visitors, and what things will keep them coming back?
- *Layout notes:* How will you present your information?
- *Tree structure:* How will you categorize and link your Web pages (or the individual components in your non-Web multimedia presentation)?

The following content outline shows one way to answer all of these criteria. It was used in the site design for the cookingwithpam.com domain.

Sample Content Outline for a Web Site

Domain Name: www.cookingwithpam.com

Objective: Provide a free recipe resource to promote cookbooks and other titles authored by Pamela Rice Hahn

Target Audience 1: Visitors who like to cook
Target Audience 2: Visitors who don't like to cook but want quick and easy recipes

Resources—Target Audience 1

Recipe pages

Reviews: Products and ingredients—generic, and also from specific suppliers
Utensils and cookware from specific suppliers
Appliances—general instructions and reviews of specific brand names
Cookbooks—written by Pamela Rice Hahn and other authors

Resources—Target Audience 2

Quick and Easy Recipe pages

Reviews:	Products and ingredients—generic, and also from specific suppliers, with emphasis on time-saving and not sacrificing quality for time
	Utensils and cookware from specific suppliers, with emphasis on time-saving benefits
	Appliances—general instructions and reviews of specific brand names with emphasis on time-saving benefits
	Cookbooks—Provide additional tips along with any reviews, plus links to related information
Layout Notes:	For the purposes of continuity, all Web pages will follow a template. Each page will follow a hierarchical structure based on the Tree Structure.

Tree Structure

Main title page:	Featured recipes, featured tips, navigation guide
Categories:	About, Bread, Baking, Chocolate, Equipment, Cookbooks, My Books, Grilling, Diabetes, Enabled, Whey, Low/Sugar-Free, Tips & Tricks

Individual recipes and related information: Linked from categories

Resources:	Site index, category index, alphabetical index, search page

Once you've addressed all of these elements, you can get down to the real work of creating content without having these little details stop you along the way.

Storyboard Strategy

A storyboard can be an effective tool for planning your online presentation. In essence, a storyboard is simply an outline with pictures that indicate the steps that will be taken along the way. Storyboarding allows you to plot your presentation out visually so that you can see how it will look at all stages.

Storyboards are often used in film or television production to provide the crew with a visual example of how the final shot should look. This way, the director's vision is represented in a graphic format that can be easily seen by the props people, lighting technicians, and everyone else involved in the process. When working with a team, these storyboards get everyone focused toward a common goal.

But even if you're not working on a team, a storyboard is still effective because it makes you think about how your presentation will be viewed graphically. It gives you the opportunity to figure out how you want each screen to look.

✍ Special Considerations

When using multimedia elements, always consider any technological challenges your readers may face. For example, if you use special technology like Macromedia Flash Player, be aware that some of your visitors might not have it installed. Make sure this sort of special technology isn't the only source of the information you're trying to present. Always offer the option of viewing your Web page as a standard HTML file.

Of course, your storyboard won't contain only pictures. Each picture should also include a written description that explains the elements in a particular section. You won't need a picture in the storyboard for every screen of your online presentation. You'll merely want to plot out the major elements, and then elaborate upon them in the accompanying text. Your storyboards can be as simple or elaborate as you'd like, from hand-drawn stick figures and written notes, to Microsoft PowerPoint–style presentations.

When creating a storyboard, the first step is to break down your presentation into individual components. If you've already been working from an outline, this should be relatively simple; just follow your outline, modifying it slightly to incorporate the visual aspects. If you haven't already done so, this is the time to start an outline. Follow the instructions for making a general outline, and simply note where you plan to include pictures. Then, elaborate upon the descriptions.

Storyboards give you the opportunity to experiment with different formats before you go through the work of fully implementing each design. This process allows you to see how your final product will be displayed, and it helps you to recognize any problems that might arise during the implementation stage. If you catch them early, you'll have the chance to fix design challenges before they become difficult to change.

✍ Scripting Audio Clips

If your multimedia piece will use sound bites or small audio clips, you'll need to script them. Remember, the written word and the spoken word are two completely different things. When people are speaking, they often bend—or entirely ignore—grammatical rules. You want your sound bites to sound natural and appealing, not stilted and artificial, so you'll need to take a slightly different approach when writing scripts for the spoken word.

Working with a Production Team

If your multimedia presentation is going to be large, you probably won't be handling it all on your own. It's likely you'll be working with an entire production team to achieve your goal. Production teams often include the following people:

- A team leader who oversees the group.
- Design specialists who are familiar with Web publishing technology.
- Writing staff, including writers, proofreaders, and copyeditors.
- Financial management staff for large projects.

- Production assistants who ensure that day-to-day tasks are completed.

The design and makeup of a production team will depend on the project scope. For very large projects, a number of people might carry out the above roles. For smaller projects, team members may don multiple hats.

The production team will break up the necessary tasks and assign them to individuals within the group. Often, frequent production meetings will be held to discuss progress and challenges. Be forthright in your dealings with the group, as you may find that they are able to offer invaluable assistance if you are having problems. Also be ready to offer your assistance when others require it.

🖎 Expanding Your Multimedia Efforts

You can apply "multimedia" concepts to other types of presentations, beyond those on the Web. For instance, office presentations done in Microsoft PowerPoint convey information through a similar approach. (The interactivity is just sometimes more limited.) Corporations can also use interactive brochures to provide information to shareholders, or as reference materials for staff training initiatives. The application combinations of multimedia writing are seemingly limitless.

Chapter 11

Journalism

Professional newspaper and magazine writers aren't the only ones who need to use journalistic techniques. Other types of writing, such as press releases or information newsletters for clubs and organizations, follow a similar format. Regardless of how you structure the beginning, the middle, and the end of any story, it always needs to include those ever-essential basics: who, what, when, where, why, and how.

The Inverted Pyramid

The "inverted pyramid" is the simplest, most commonly used story structure. Think of the "inverted pyramid" as an upside-down triangle, with the narrow tip of less important information pointing downward (at the end of the story) and the broad base of newsworthy details running across the top (the beginning of the story).

This journalistic format is the most practical, because stories need to be a particular length to fill up a predetermined amount of space in a newspaper or magazine. In order to make such stories "fit," edits must be done, often under severe deadline pressure. A story written in inverted pyramid format can be easily edited by trimming it one paragraph at a time, from the bottom up, until the story is the proper length. When the least important information runs at the end of the story, the editor making cuts can do so confidently, knowing nothing that is integral to the story will be lost.

Types of Leads

The first paragraph of a news story is known as the lead. Often, the lead is one long sentence that summarizes the facts of the news story in order of most newsworthy to least newsworthy. This helps the reader know at a glance what the story will be about. The lead also sets the structure for the rest of the story.

Following are some of the most frequently used journalistic leads:

The Story Summary Lead

> Because of concerns over the growing menace of the West Nile virus and the need to educate physicians on newly developed diagnosis techniques, doctors from the Center for Disease Control (CDC) met today with representatives from the American Family Physicians Society.

The News Lead

The news lead usually describes specific actions.

> In one of the most gruesome incidents in years, a Palestinian suicide bomber grabbed an Israeli child from his mother's arms before killing himself, the child, and ten others when he detonated the bomb he had strapped to his waist.

The Quote Lead

The quote lead begins with a directly attributed quote. It's especially effective when the quote makes the reader automatically want to know more—if it motivates the reader to ask questions.

> "I felt the crunch before the tingle."

The Description Lead

Often used at the beginning of feature articles, this lead provides a descriptive image of the feature's subject.

> **Looking out of place wearing a tie, as evidenced by the rash around his collar that seemingly grew brighter with each word he spoke, farmer Jacob Miller sat stiff in his chair as he addressed the members of the congressional committee.**

Tips for Conducting Interviews

Whether you're talking to someone in person, or interviewing him or her over the phone, there are a number of things you should do to prepare for the interview and during the interview itself.

1. Do your homework. Learn about your subject in advance. If you're interviewing a businessperson, visit his or her company or look at its Web site. Take good notes as you do research, and highlight any instances where you might need clarification.
2. Have open-ended questions ready in advance. Prepare more than you'll have time to ask—in anticipation of the interview going well and the subject of your interview asking you to stay and talk longer. Advance preparation also demonstrates that you've done your homework, and that you respect the interviewee's time.
3. Be courteous. Be on time, and if the interview takes place in person, dress appropriately. When you introduce yourself, have a business card or paper with contact information ready.
4. Break the ice. Allow a brief period of time to get to know one another before you start asking questions. Ask the subject of the interview if he or she has any questions about you or the interview protocol before you begin.
5. Ask for permission to tape the interview. Have your taping equipment—with an adequate fresh battery supply and appropriately sized tapes—ready in advance. Also have a notepad and pen or pencil ready so you can take notes. (If the interview is in person,

also take notes about the atmosphere and any body language.) Never rely on your memory alone.

6. Confirm and clarify, and then confirm again. Ask for proper spellings for any names or terms about which you're unsure. Confirm that you have the correct spelling of your interviewee. Get clarification on any new terms brought up during your discussion.

7. End the interview on friendly terms. Thank your subject. Ask for a convenient time to contact that person again, should you have questions or need clarification.

8. Transcribe your notes as soon as possible. Don't let too much time pass before you organize your notes; you want to do so while your overall impressions and the facts are fresh in your mind.

Using Direct and Paraphrased Quotes

A direct quote repeats what the subject of your interview said exactly, and is surrounded by quotation marks. Otherwise, when you paraphrase something that was said, quotation marks aren't used—although they are sometimes used around a quoted portion of a paraphrased segment to add emphasis.

> **The preacher looked out over the crowd, took a deep breath, and commented about how glad he was to see so many "faithful followers" in attendance.**

Direct quotes are used:

- To answer how, what, who, or why questions.
- To include exact or official information, especially when it's important that it comes from an obviously authoritative voice.
- When the interviewee's language is particularly descriptive.

Press Releases

Much of what you see or read in the news doesn't just occur there because news agencies have battalions of reporters off doing investigative journalism and tracking down information all the time. Reporters usually turn up to cover an event because they first learned about it from a press release.

A press release is a written announcement that can be used to broadcast any number of events, from a fundraising dinner to a new product release to a job promotion.

A press release that doesn't require immediate attention can be delivered in person or by mail; otherwise, for late-breaking news, fax or e-mail distribution is also acceptable.

Unless it's via e-mail, a press release should be typed on letterhead (or other professionally designed paper). The proper format also includes:

- Contact information, including the name and daytime phone number of the person.
- Release date (traditionally "For Immediate Release"—although some now consider that line superfluous; "For Release On (or After) <Date>" can also be used).
- Headline (centered and in bold type).
- Dateline (the city name in all capital letters, followed by date of release).
- The body, or the actual news release itself, should contain the essential how, who, what, where, when, and why information, double-spaced on one side of 8½" × 11" paper.
- If the release extends beyond one page, center and type "(CONTINUED)" or "(MORE)" at the bottom of the page.
- Number consecutive pages by placing the release title or a key word from the release title and the page number flush left at the margin at the top of the page.
- Center one of the following to indicate the end of the release: # # #, – 30 – , (END).

Sample Press Release

FOR IMMEDIATE RELEASE   Contact: Tony Rice
                                           Creative Visions Club
                                           555 That Boulevard
                                           Celina, OH 45822
                                           Phone: (555) 555-5555
                                           Fax: (555) 555-5556
                                           E-mail: tony@domain.com

THE CREATIVE VISIONS CLUB TO HOST
SECOND ANNUAL ANIMATIONFEST

CELINA, April 1—Over the weekend of April 6–8, local animators will once again gather at the Florence Convention Center in downtown Celina for the Second Annual Animationfest.

Joining local artists and scriptwriters will be nationally known figures such as keynote speaker Jemma Smith, creator of RubbaDubbaHubba, and seminar instructor Taylor Sutton, the force behind Wild Animal Extravaganza. [List other important event data]

"We're proud to once again be having so many distinguished artisans teaming up with local talent," said Tony Rice, president of the local Creative Visions Club. "We already have more than a thousand people registered to attend the classes and seminars," he continued, adding, "but there's still time for anyone who's interested to participate," indicating a few registration slots are still open.

This year's Animationfest will conclude on Sunday, April 8, with an open house and reception, open to the public—although registration at the door will be limited to the first thousand people who attend. Animationfest participants will be available to autograph merchandise—like special video packages, prints, and animation cells.

All profits from the event go to support the Creative Visions Club mentoring program.

Chapter 12

Writing Creative Nonfiction

Not all nonfiction is as dry as technical writing, as esoteric as academic essays, or as utilitarian as business writing. Writing many types of nonfiction can be quite creative. Humor, reviews, personal essays, and memoirs are all genres that allow you to individualize your writing. Understanding these forms will help you to add further dimension and depth to your writing skills. This chapter not only provides descriptions to help you learn about the writing choices available, it also gives you suggestions for adapting your personalized stories to meet your writing needs.

Humor

Everybody loves a good laugh. Laughter is therapeutic, and it's even more satisfying when you're able to make others laugh. Before you start writing your own material, you need to know a bit about humor theories and what makes people laugh.

For starters, humor can be an effective (and sometimes less risky) way to show things like ambivalence, incongruity, surprise, or superiority. Such effects can be achieved with wordplay that evokes emotion, uses exaggeration, conveys disguised hostility, presents a surprise twist, or employs humor aimed at popular "targets"—authority, family, finances, sex, technology, and so on. Other comedic formulas that are sure to make people laugh include double entendres (words with double meanings, the second of which usually has a sexual connotation); incongruity (using logical ideas that result in an unconventional conclusion); insult humor; one-liners ("Take my wife, please!"); and paired phrases (complete-the-phrase jokes like: "Today it was so cold that _____").

Comedic Genres

Humor comes in all shapes and sizes, and there's something for everyone. Some of the most popular, and adaptable, comedic genres are as follows.

Anecdotes

Anecdotes are short narratives about a humorous incident.

> A few weeks before her fifth birthday, my niece Jemma ran through the room, picked up her mom's purse on the way, and grabbed the cordless phone. Her mother asked her, "What in the world do you think you're doing?"
>
> Jemma answered: "I want to get you this mop I just saw on TV and the guy told me I only have five minutes to order it!"

Cartoons

Cartoons are illustrated, single-thought jokes. They are among the most difficult types of humor to write—it's challenging to get a comedic point across in a single illustration accompanied by just a sentence or two. Randy Glasbergen (*www.glasbergen.com*), whose *The Better Half* comic strip appears in many newspapers, is also well known for his cartoons, many of which run in corporate newsletters.

Comic Strips

Comic strips are similar to cartoons, but include more than one "scene." The standard cartoon format consists of three panels, but this is by no means a hard and fast rule. Comic strips give the creator the luxury of building humor slowly, setting the reader up for the punch line in the final panel. Because there's more space, they also allow for a greater variety of characters in a single work. Examples of well-known comic strips like Charles Schultz's *Peanuts* and Scott Adams' *Dilbert* can be seen at *www.comics.com*. Other writer-artists publish their works on their own sites, such as *Squinkers* comic, at *www.squinkers.com*.

Humor Columns

Dave Barry is probably one of the best known and widest read humor columnists working today. Whether he's writing about current events or one of his personal experiences, he blends phrases his readers have now come to expect—like "I'm not making this up," and "a good name for a rock band"—with an exaggerated reporting style that always seems to make people laugh. Many writers take advantage of magazines and Web sites that publish similar columns to establish publicity for their other works. For example, Southern humor book author Ed Williams (*www.edwilliams.com*) self-syndicates his column to a number of Georgia newspapers. The Blue Rose Bouquet (*www.blueroses.com*) reprints the works of newspaper columnists like Randy Shore, who writes about his children.

Parody

A parody is a work of humor that imitates the style of a particular source. For example, writers for *The Onion* (*www.theonion.com*) combine satire and newspaper parody. *The Onion* is known for all sorts of parodies, from human relations stories, to pseudo news stories that have even fooled members of the foreign press.

Puns

These dual-meaning jokes can induce laugh-out-loud humor. More often, these subtle—and sometimes not-so-subtle—plays on words usually elicit groans. A pun takes a common word or phrase, and skewers it enough to change its meaning; such as, a review for a bad German restaurant that advises reader only to go there for the "wurst of times" or a headline that proclaims "Udder Relief for the Dairy Industry."

Puns can be one-liners:

> **Kiwifruit tart is a berry good dessert.**

The answers to riddles:

> **Do you know what they call ushers at the Vatican?**
> **Papal People Seaters**

They can also deliver a story's punch line. Take this example, from The Blue Rose Bouquet (*www.blueroses.com*).

> **Billions of dollars in research grants had already been spent for the studies conducted by the best and brightest physics, psychiatric, medical, and other scientific researchers across the country when a psychology professor at Harvard arrived at the conclusion that perhaps everyone was putting too much energy into the project. He argued that minds were too easily distracted by everyday life and other body functions. Therefore—at the conclusion of another grant-funded study, of course—it was determined that because extra bodies were unnecessary for the project, tenured professors everywhere severed the heads of all doctoral candidates, hooked them to life support systems, and assigned them the sole purpose of working on a solution to the problem. Still no one could arrive at the desired results. Finally, one scientist invited everyone to gather up the heads and bring them to a conference at Cambridge, because "I'm sure if we all put our heads together, we can come up with a solution."**

Satire

Satire is humor that uses sarcasm, irony, derision, and sharpened wit to lampoon human experience. The more seriously a segment of society seems to take itself, the bigger a target it becomes for satirical skewering.

Certain subjects lend themselves particularly well to satire: educational systems, politics, pop culture, and religion, to name a few.

> **A nationally recognized teachers union announced today that they'd oppose any legislation asking for teacher certification testing, stating that tests are not a reliable and accurate way to gauge proficiency. Students across the nation welcomed this news, adapting that philosophy as they put in a bid to establish their own union.**

Targeted Humor

Niche market humor makes fun of or parodies a particular topic, such as religion, pets, and sports. For example, knowing that overweight women are often popular targets for jokes, there's a niche humor market that runs counter to the usual, run-of-the-mill fat jokes. Instead, the authors make fun of themselves, celebrating their abundance, so to speak. Rather than be the brunt of fat jokes, this brand of humor (like that found at *www.blossomfuller.com*) turns the tables and celebrates size in an unconventional way.

How and Where to Use Humor

Even in cases where your primary goal is to convey information, you can still use humor to get your point across. Chris Pirillo's Lockergnome.com is a great example—it's a newsletter and Web site that dispenses technical computer information with a humorous bent.

The key to using humor in various types of writing is directing its meaning and shaping it so that it fits the purpose of your message. For example, the anecdote example featured earlier in this chapter about the young girl rushing to order the mop for her mother within the five-minute deadline could be recounted in the introduction to an advertising promotion planning meeting. After sharing the anecdote, the speaker could follow with a transition such as:

> **"That story illustrates the good and bad news of one television advertising campaign. An effective infomercial advertisement is one that reaches its target audience, and convinces**

people to act right away. The good news is that somebody who heard the message was motivated to act. The bad news is that five-year-olds are not the target audience."

As long as you keep your audience in mind and target your humor so that it's in good taste and appropriate for the occasion, humor can be an effective way to grab—and maintain—your audience's attention.

Reviews

You already know that who, what, where, and when are important aspects of informative writing; however, when it comes to writing a review, the other two elements—why and how—are especially important. A review is your assessment of a product or service. You establish the first four elements when you explain who is reviewing the product (sometimes an unspoken understanding), what is being reviewed, and where and when the product was used. But describing those elements is only effective if you also give details about why and how you reached your conclusions.

When writing reviews, share your personal experiences. Why do you recommend a product? How has it made your life better?

Before you write your own reviews, first become a reviewer of other reviews. Study them to determine which ones are most informative. Figure out what those authors did (or didn't do) to make their reviews effective.

✍ Support Your Opinions with Facts

Your review should be your opinion, supported by those facts that caused you to form that opinion. A statement like "I recommend you buy this book" is only effective if the reader knows why you feel that way.

Unless you're establishing your own review medium—like the movie review site at *www.reelcriticism.com*—you'll need to follow the dictates of the publisher for whom you're writing the review. Some publications prefer reviews written in the first person ("I like this product because . . ."). Others prefer second person ("You will find this product helpful because . . .").

Personal Essays

Personal essays are opinion pieces that include the author's personal perspective, reactions, and opinions on a particular subject. Anything about which the author cares deeply (although not necessarily that about which he or she cares seriously) is an appropriate subject for a personal essay. It's an essay about what you feel, written so that the reader recognizes what you believe and why you feel that way.

Personal essays range from political commentary (opinion pieces) to humor columns like those written by Dave Barry to anecdotal musings. Personal narratives are often as effective whether they're read by the reader or read aloud by the author in the form of a speech or radio commentary.

The Hook

The hook is the device you use to get your reader's attention. In personal essays, a good hook can come in a variety of forms:

Sample Hook: Description of a Person or Setting

My computer monitor has a Winnie the Pooh Band-Aid on it.

The opening line to "Life's Bumps and Band-Aids" is from *Rhymes and Reasons*
(unpublished book of personal essays by Pamela Rice Hahn)
Copyright © 1999–2003 Pamela Rice Hahn. Used by permission.

Sample Hook: Description That Involves the Senses

In a nursing home, it's possible to get overwhelmed by the ever-present odors. Sweet citrus disinfectant does little to mask them. Chlorine scent clings to bleached linens. Perfumes and aftershaves worn by residents, visitors, and employees leave intermittent wafts of fragrance in their wake. And, always, worst of all, is the stench of functioning and malfunctioning body processes. Fluids and wastes. Their trail rises above all else. It permeates the air. It penetrates the very essence of that environment, becoming a fixture. Tangible.

The opening lines to "We Never Lose Hope" are from *Rhymes and Reasons*
(unpublished book of personal essays by Pamela Rice Hahn).
Copyright © 1999–2003 Pamela Rice Hahn. Used by permission.

Sample Hook: Question or Questions

Men. And what about those eyelash-batting, collagen-injected, vacuumed-thighed, plunging necklined, surgically augmented jiggle machines who make them feel like boys? Don't they just make your butt dimple with envy?

The opening lines to "The Seduction Samba" are from *Rhymes and Reasons* (unpublished book of personal essays by Pamela Rice Hahn). Copyright © 1999–2003 Pamela Rice Hahn. Used by permission.

Sample Hook: Quotation

A friend's comment probably sums it up best: After the initial flames die down on the charcoal of the marriage, the real cooking is done on the glowing embers.

The opening lines to "The Comfortable Familiarity of Marriage" are from *Rhymes and Reasons* (unpublished book of personal essays by Pamela Rice Hahn). Copyright © 1999–2003 Pamela Rice Hahn. Used by permission.

Sample Hook: Statement Intended to Introduce Controversy

The way I figure it, there are men out there overlooking the opportunity to find the perfect mistress.

The opening lines to "PWC*: An Untapped Market" are from *Rhymes and Reasons* (unpublished book of personal essays by Pamela Rice Hahn). Copyright © 1999–2003 Pamela Rice Hahn. Used by permission.

Sample Hook: A Statement That Will Either Be Supported or Disputed

Today, it seems, everybody wants to be a victim.

From the Introduction to *Rhymes and Reasons* (unpublished book of personal essays by Pamela Rice Hahn). Copyright © 1999–2003 Pamela Rice Hahn. Used by permission.

Ensure Accuracy

Always make sure your supporting facts are accurate. If you make a factual error and someone calls it into question, you could be courting negative publicity that will affect your credibility.

Make Connections

Even if you're writing about global issues, introducing a personal example—or at least one "closer to home"—helps the reader relate better to the issue. If the opposite is true and you're writing your opinions about the increase in local spousal abuse statistics, for example, citing a wider range of statistics would help to establish a broader perspective.

Include Fictional Elements

Dialog, characterization, and setting details are ways to introduce constructive changes into your essay. They increase the readability of your essay by giving you a way to alter the pace, and providing you with devices to use to avoid beginning every sentence with "I."

Involve the Reader

When you only state your opinions about something in order to get it off your chest, you're not writing an essay—you're simply ranting. Instead, find ways to take a step back from the immediacy of your own feelings and introduce elements that will connect with your reader.

✍ *Fact Versus Opinion*

Academic essays, like those discussed in Chapter 6, are written objectively and include more facts than opinion. Personal essays, on the other hand, are far more subjective and generally include more opinions than facts.

Memoirs

Similar to a personal essay, a memoir is an author's autobiographical description of events. Although they can be shorter, memoirs are often written in longer, book-length format. (One famous recent memoir is Frank McCourt's *Angela's Ashes*.) Whether intended for publication or not, memoir writing is a vehicle for revisiting parts of the past and recording those events as a means of self-discovery or to preserve those memories for future generations.

Don't think that memoirs are synonymous with autobiographies, however. An autobiography is a factual telling of an entire life. A memoir doesn't necessarily focus on a chronological description of an entire life, but rather on the author's *impressions* of his or her life. In fact, a memoir's description is often limited to a single event. A memoir allows for some leeway, if not creative license, on the author's part, and therefore isn't something that's heavily researched. It's more about the author's recollections and perceptions about details and relationships than it is about specifically recorded events.

A memoir can be something as simple as a written impression about a memory evoked by a photo in a scrapbook. It can range from a one-sentence description that begins, "I remember that on the day this photograph was taken . . ." to something as long as the author feels is necessary to record the event.

Chapter 13

Writing for Publication

There are certain basics for writing fiction and nonfiction pieces that you should understand if you want to try your hand at writing for publication. You need to know how to present your piece properly and how to get it into the hands of the right people. Manuscript style preferences and submission standards vary from publisher to publisher—and even by imprint within larger publishing conglomerates. Submission standards for fiction also differ from those for nonfiction. Keep in mind the content needs and expectations for general interest publications vary significantly from those of academic, literary, religious, and scientific periodicals.

Obtaining Publisher Guidelines

Publisher guidelines contain specific information about the kinds of work the publisher buys from authors. In addition, the guidelines feature important information about how to format and submit your manuscript. Almost all publishers have guideline sheets available on request. All you need to do to obtain them is send a simple, straightforward letter. There's no need to go into detail about your writing project in this letter. Your only purpose is obtaining those guidelines.

Sample Request for Publisher Guidelines

Ms. Janet Worth
Acquisitions Editor
ABC Publisher
12115 5th Ave.
New York, NY 10112

Dear Ms. Worth:

Enclosed please find a SASE. I would like a copy of your writer's guidelines.

Thank you,

David L. Herbert

Sending Query Letters

A query letter introduces you and your work to a publisher or an agent. Pay close attention to each publisher's requirements (as outlined in the writer's guidelines you receive from that publisher) to determine whether the publisher requires a complete manuscript, an outline with sample chapters, or only a query letter outlining your proposed manuscript. You might be required to submit any of these, to gauge a publisher's interest in your project. You'll probably be asked to submit more detailed information when and if an agent is willing to represent your work or a publisher wants to consider your book for publication. If a publisher doesn't publish specific submission guidelines, just send a query letter to inquire about the publisher's preferences.

Keep in mind that some publishers won't accept submissions from unrepresented authors—you may need to find an agent first.

✍ No Flying Blind

Always direct your query letter to an actual person. Call the publisher or agency to inquire as to whom you should direct your query, asking the person you speak with to confirm the spelling of the first and last names. Even when the appropriate name is listed in a writer's market guide, it's still a good idea to call, just to confirm things.

Sample Publisher Query Letter

Query Letter
Ms. Janet Worth
Acquisitions Editor
ABC Publisher
5555 Fifth Avenue
New York, NY 10112

Dear Ms. Worth:

I have recently completed a mystery novel entitled "Lurker@Heart." It is a cyber-thriller that investigates the recent popularity of online chat rooms and the potential problems that can arise from visiting them.

I can provide you either with the complete manuscript or with a synopsis and sample chapters, whichever you prefer.

Enclosed please find a SASE for your reply.

Thank you,

David L. Herbert

Mr. A. Dealmaker
XYZ Literary Agency
555 Fifth Avenue
New York, NY 10116

Dear Mr. Dealmaker:

I have recently completed a mystery novel entitled "Lurker@Heart." It is a cyber-thriller that investigates the recent popularity of online chat rooms and the potential problems that can arise from visiting them.

I am currently seeking representation for this work. May I forward the manuscript to you? Or do you prefer a synopsis and sample chapters?

Enclosed please find a SASE for your reply.

Thank you.

Sincerely,

David L. Hebert

Formatting Your Manuscript

In addition to following a publisher or agent's specific submission requirements, there are also some basic formatting guidelines to which you should adhere. For starters, manuscripts should always be double-spaced. This makes it much easier to read, and also allows room for agents or editors to make changes or add comments in the margins. Your manuscript should be single-sided as well. Think of those poor editorial assistants—photocopying a double-sided manuscript can be so tedious! And don't try to save paper by extending your margins.

Remember, editors are people who read for a living. Make your manuscript as easy on their eyes as possible by following these rules:

- Use 1″ margins on all sides. Check your word processor's default settings; you may need to modify them to meet a particular publisher's requirement.
- Include the title of your work, your contact information, and your agent's contact information on your title page.
- List your name as you'd like it to read for your byline. If you write under your real name, you obviously don't need to include a byline; however, if you plan to use a pseudonym, let the publisher know.
- Start the body of your manuscript on page one, after you list contact information (you don't need to number the beginning of your story as page two).
- Don't hole-punch, staple, or otherwise bind the manuscript. A large butterfly clip is sometimes fine (unless specifically prohibited in the publisher guidelines), but the manuscript pages themselves should remain unmarred.
- Add a header that includes your last name, the manuscript title, and a page number to each subsequent page. If you have a very long title, you can use a portion of it; just be sure your abbreviated version will trigger an editor's memory if your manuscript pages get separated.

Some publishers like the page numbering to appear centered at the bottom of the page, but this is the exception to the rule and seldom used. (Manuscripts submitted electronically as a word-processing program file often don't require page numbering, either as a header or footer, at all.) If the guidelines do not give page header or page numbering specifics, use this format, flush right, at the top of the page:

Hahn/The Only Writing Book You'll Ever Need/Page 2

Of course, some publishers might require variations to these general guidelines. For example, if a publisher uses a "blind" editorial evaluation team, editors will read manuscripts without knowing which agents have submitted them or who the authors are. If this is the case, the publisher will request that your contact information appears only on a separate title page, and nowhere else on the manuscript. (Your header, then, would contain only the title and the page number.)

Creating Your Author Bio

Many publishers will ask that you send a short biographical statement with your manuscript. This gives them background as they're reading your work, and it can also be used for promotional purposes or even to draft a bio blurb that will appear on the back of your book.

Your bio should include the following information.

- Your background experience: What kinds of relevant things have you done in your life? What can you include in your bio that will show the publishers and the editors your background and past experiences?
- Your educational experience: Do you have a Ph.D. or other titles that lend credibility and demonstrate your expertise in your subject area? Credentials can help to sell books. Have you completed any training programs related to the field you're writing about? Even if your educational experience is unrelated, include it. It's good background for the people who must publicize and market your book.
- Past writing credits: Including information shows editors, publicists, and publishers that they're working with someone who has experience.

You might also include any awards or fellowships you've received, as well as significant sales information or review quotes on your previous works.

Your bio should be short; a page—or about 250 words—is sufficient. (It's okay to use 1½-line spacing instead of double spacing on the biography only, if that's what it takes to hit that one-page goal.) Some publishers might request more detailed information, while others might want a bio of no more than a few sentences. If the publisher has required specifications, follow those closely. Write your biographical statement in the third person.

The following introductory lines from a biographical statement come from the Web site of a Canadian colleague. Unless it's accompanying a humor submission, it might be a little too tongue-in-cheek to send to a publisher; however, it shows you how one author conveys his information:

> David L. Hebert came into this world on December 24, 1970, and just like Gracie Allen, was so surprised he didn't speak for almost two years. It was a burst of enthusiasm from which he still hasn't quite recovered.

The style of your author biography should be appropriate for the style of the book you're pitching—humorous, if appropriate, or cerebral for more serious works.

The Essentials of a Solid Book Proposal

As mentioned earlier in this chapter, some publishers and agents expect to first receive a query letter before you send your proposal. Remember to consult publisher or agent guidelines before you submit a proposal. There are several proposal formats that are acceptable.

Your Cover Letter

A cover letter for a book proposal can be longer than one page because it includes the "pitch" for your book. Format this letter as you would a formal business letter, using single spacing with two-line feeds between each paragraph. Introduce your proposal by giving your proposed book title, followed by a one-sentence description of your proposed book. Next, present other essential information about the book in synopsis format, explaining such things as:

- The potential audience for the book.
- The tone of the book (humorous, instructional, exposé).
- The type of book (hardcover, trade paperback, etc.).
- Your expertise (why you're the perfect person to write the book).

- Any other experience (e.g., media) that will help market the book.
- A brief description of the supporting documents you're including with the proposal.

Sample Cover Letter

Ms. Regan
555 Fifth Avenue
New York, NY 10112

Dear Ms. Regan:

More than a million people now work with widgets on a daily basis and that number is growing with each passing day. The Wonderful Widget is a book that would work in either hardcover or as a trade paperback. The book will address the phenomena of America's fascination with the widget, defining the many aspects of what makes the widget an essential part of so many households. The book will walk the reader step-by-step through the information necessary to know, appreciate, and then use the widget.

I worked as Mr. Michael Bishop's personal assistant for more than ten years and have observed the evolution of the widget—from concept to working model to marketing phenomena. Now, as marketing director for the company, I have appeared as his spokesperson on news programs on all major networks, when Mr. Bishop has been unable to appear himself because of scheduling conflicts. Mr. Bishop promises his full cooperation on the development of this book. I'll have full access to his notes and supporting documents.

I'm including my proposed table of contents for this book (along with chapter descriptions), plus information on competing titles, my author biography (this isn't my first book), a sample chapter, and publicity and promotion suggestions for the book.

Thank you for your time and consideration. I look forward to discussing this project with you at your convenience.

Sincerely,

Jodi Cornelius

Some authors prefer to forego a cover letter and begin with a cover page, followed by a two- to three-page "pitch" for the book. This book pitch contains essentially the same elements that go into a cover letter, except it doesn't include the editor and publisher (or agent) information and greeting. Instead, it begins by repeating the proposed book title, followed by a one-sentence description. The book pitch, like the rest of the proposal, should be double-spaced. If an agent will be submitting your work to potential publishers, be sure to write your book pitch in third person.

Your Cover Page

Your first task is writing a great title for your proposed book. Once you've done that, on your cover page, print the title in all uppercase letters, centered in the upper third of a blank page; use double-spacing if the title is more than one line. Centered and double-spaced below the title, use upper and lowercase letters to print your name. In the bottom third of the page, tabbed near the right margin, type your name, address, and phone number (or your agent's name, address, and phone number). If you include both, be sure to identify the agent information. This information can be single- or double-spaced, depending on the amount of information you include.

✍ Include a SASE

Whenever you send a letter to a publisher, always include a self-addressed, stamped envelope, known as a SASE. The SASE is an expected courtesy from the author. Publishers cannot afford to respond to all mail they receive from prospective writers, and without a SASE, your letter might hit the garbage pail instead of the "response" pile.

Your Proposed Table of Contents

Writing a proposed table of contents involves working the concept for your book into an outline of sorts, only in this instance you'll list chapter titles, followed by one-paragraph descriptions of what you intend to cover in that chapter. A well-written table of contents description shows editors that you know how to organize a book.

Sample Initial Part of a Table of Contents

The Only Writing Book You'll Ever Need
Chapter 1: Laying the Right Foundation
This chapter will review the basics for all good writing. An effective written message needs to answer the questions Who, What, When, Where, Why, and How, and it also needs a solid beginning, middle, and end. It will also troubleshoot some common mistakes many writers make, such as improper subject/verb agreement and passive voice. Finally, in a brief section, this chapter will address developing solid editing and proofreading, reminding writers not to rely on spellcheck to catch all mistakes.

Copyright Concerns

If you are considering submitting your writing for publication, it would behoove you to learn the basics of copyright law. Copyright gives the owner the right to reproduce the work in any form, to make derivative works based on the original work, and to distribute copies of the work. Usually, the owner of the work is the person who creates the work. In literary terms, the work can be anything from a short story, novel, play, or poem, to a nonfiction article, a screenplay, or virtually any other form of written communication.

Copyright law strikes a balance between two competing interests. On the one hand, it encourages authors and artists to create work and it ensures that they will be able to receive adequate compensation for their efforts. On the other hand, the doctrine of fair use serves to balance out the potential monopoly created by copyright law by allowing people to use certain aspects of literary and other works without infringing on the copyright. (Fair use will be discussed in detail later in this chapter.)

🖎 *A Matter of Originality*

In order to qualify for copyright, a work must be original. That doesn't necessarily mean it has to be original in the innovative sense; originality simply requires that the work's creator expended some effort in creating it.

It's important to understand that copyright protects only the actual expression of an idea, not the idea itself. Ideas are for the benefit of society, and therefore must be free. Think about Einstein's famous formula. While he could have claimed copyright in the words he used to express the idea, he could never have copyrighted the idea of $e = mc^2$.

This distinction is inextricably tied to one of the basic qualifications of copyright law: In order to claim copyright in a literary work, it must be fixed. This simply means that the work must be written down. Since only the expression of an idea is protected, a thing must actually be expressed in some way before it can be protected.

🖎 *Work-for-Hire Agreements*

Sometimes, a publisher will commission a specific work. In such circumstances, the publisher and author may establish a work-for-hire agreement in which the publisher, not the author, owns the copyright.

It used to be that a literary work had to be registered with the copyright office to assert a claim; this is no longer the case, and copyright begins at the moment of fixation. As soon as you write something down, or type it into a word-processing document and save it to your hard drive, you are the copyright owner.

Duration of Copyright and Public Domain

In order to provide authors with long-term protection of their works, the current term of copyright protection extends from the date of the work's creation until seventy years after the author's death. After this point, the work enters the public domain, and can be copied freely without regard to copyright infringement.

Unless the terms of the contract specify otherwise, in the case of works commissioned under work-for-hire agreements, the copyright will last for ninety-five years after the date of publication. If the work is unpublished, the copyright of commissioned works under a work-for-hire agreement lasts 120 years.

✍ Up with the Times

Copyright law has had some catching up to do because of technology. It currently includes works that aren't actually set out on paper. Works stored on computer hard drives are fine, as are documents kept in a personal digital assistant: As long as the work is stored and can be retrieved, it is protected by copyright.

Works created earlier than 1998 will enter the public domain earlier, depending on the original date of publication. This is still of historical interest when trying to determine when a particular work from the past is to enter the public domain, but any works created after 1999 will follow the rules outlined above.

Collective Works

Sometimes, articles or short stories are collected and published together in an anthology. As such, although many of the individual components will still carry their own individual copyright, owned by the author, copyright also exists for the anthology. This means that no one else can compile the same works together and publish them. In most cases, unless the contract agreement specifies otherwise, the original author still retains the rights to the individual stories or articles.

Collaboration Agreements

Two authors may own an interest in the copyright of a work if both authors contribute to the creation of the work. The contribution, however, must be relatively substantial and involve a significant amount of actual work. Merely suggesting ideas or titles does not make a claim for joint authorship.

If you collaborate with someone, it is essential to have a collaboration agreement to govern the work. In such an agreement, you can specify which authors receive what percentage. When it comes down to determining the interests in a court case, the split may be fifty-fifty, so if you don't want that to happen, it's a good idea to have a collaboration agreement right from the start. These agreements clearly specify each author's respective copyright interests, while also protecting individual legal interests regarding matters of payment, expected contributions, and so forth. There are a slew of sample collaboration agreements available on the Internet. You can use any form you like, as long as it addresses the following five points:

1. The parties to the agreement, with full contact information clearly spelled out.
2. The contribution that each party is expected to make.
3. The agreed ownership split.
4. Provisions for advance and royalty division.
5. A clause that stipulates the name of the literary agent to be used, if applicable.

Selling or Licensing Your Copyright

Although they are relatively intangible, copyrights, trademarks, and patents are all forms of intellectual property. As property, all of these things can be transferred, licensed, or sold.

A license merely grants another party permission to use the copyright. In many cases, it also allows the licensee (or the person who buys the license from you) to enter into legal action against third parties who infringe upon the work. Publication is, in a sense, a licensing situation, where, for agreed-upon terms, you allow the publisher to print and promote your work. After your agreement with the publisher has expired, you are free to license the work over again.

Many authors talk about "selling" their reprint rights, but this is a bit of a misnomer. Sure, you get paid for reprints, but usually, you still own the copyright. If you truly were to sell your copyright, you would have no subsequent interest in it. If someone offers to "buy" your work, read your agreement carefully so that you are aware of the nature of the transaction. Make sure that you aren't actually permanently selling your copyright interest if that isn't your intention. When in doubt, enlist an attorney's services.

Fair Use

The doctrine of fair use was not originally a part of copyright law; it developed slowly through a number of court decisions. It is now an official part of the copyright law as enacted by legislation. This principle sets the parameters regarding what use other people can make of a copyrighted work before they must secure permission (or risk infringing the copyright).

✍ *Work Done While Under Employment*

Depending on the scope of the work and the nature of the employment, an employee who creates a work while under the employment of another person may find that the employer owns the work. If you work for someone and routinely create written works in the scope of your job, check your employment agreement.

Unfortunately, the lines drawn are not always that clear. There is no set number of words, percentage, or any other clearly delineated factor to determine how much information can be used. This is determined through subjective analysis, based on the use to which the copyrighted work is put.

This next bulleted list is culled from the 1961 *Report of the Register of Copyrights on the General Revision of the U.S. Copyright Law.* The wording is verbatim; the only change is that the individual examples have been broken down for easier reading. It will give you an idea of the government's approach to the doctrine of fair use. Fair use allows:

- Quotation of excerpts in a review or criticism for purposes of illustration or comment.
- Quotation of short passages in a scholarly or technical work, for illustration or clarification of the author's observations.
- Use in a parody of some of the content of the work parodied.
- Summary of an address or article, with brief quotations, in a news report.
- Reproduction by a library of a portion of a work to replace part of a damaged copy.
- Reproduction by a teacher or student of a small part of a work to illustrate a lesson.
- Reproduction of a work in legislative or judicial proceedings or reports; incidental and fortuitous reproduction, in a newsreel or broadcast, of a work located in the scene of an event being reported.

The doctrine of fair use tries to strike a balance between the copyright owner's interests and the interests of society at large to benefit by additional information being produced. To determine the scope of the doctrine of fair use, section 107 of the Copyright Act sets out four criteria to consider:

1. The purpose and nature of the use of the copyrighted material. Is the reproduction being used for a commercial use? Is it for non-profit or educational uses? Is it being used for scientific research? Is it being used for the purposes of criticism or commentary? All of these questions shed light on the analysis of the first point. The more commercial the use is, the less likely it will be considered "fair." Uses such as teaching and research are given more breadth. The nature of criticism and commentary usually requires that a portion of the work being considered be quoted to some extent; as long as the reproduction isn't too substantial in the context of the criticism, that use should be considered fair, too.

2. The nature of the copyrighted work. Is the work that is being reproduced merely factual in nature? Or is it something that came from the author's imagination? Is it something that was

written for the betterment of society, or is it purely for entertainment purposes? Is it something that was written specifically for commercial exploitation? The nature of the work being produced is as important as the use to which it will be put.

3. The amount of the work reproduced, relative to the copyrighted work as a whole. If you're reproducing most of a work, you're probably on your way to infringement, and you should either find another way of doing things or seek permission from the copyright owner. In the professional world, obtaining permission is sometimes referred to as "clearance." It's always a good idea to get permission if you're using a poem or a song, since even one line can amount to a substantial portion of the work. With other types of work, a paragraph or two is probably okay. Condensing an original work into a précis (a condensed, summarized form of the original work) would probably also be an infringement, because you are reproducing a substantial part.

4. The potential market impact and how it may affect the copyrighted work. If a work is out of print and not commercially available, reproduction of some part (even a relatively substantial part, depending on the circumstances) will probably be considered fair. If the copyright owner is in a position to charge a fee for material use, this tips the balance out of the realm of fair use, but this must be considered alongside the other factors. If a work is commercially available, your use may replace the need for a consumer to purchase the original work, and therefore any reproduction you attempt will probably not be considered fair.

If, after considering the above factors, you decide that your proposed use would not fall within the fair use doctrine, you can always contact the copyright owner to obtain permission. In some cases, payment of fees is required; however, a great number of authors are happy to see that their works are being cited and readily grant permission.

Quoting or Referring to Experts

Because copyright protection does not extend to the ideas expressed in a work, you can safely state the ideas and conclusions of others without regard to existing copyright. Copyright cannot be used as a monopoly for an idea, so these types of quotes can be used as long as the usage does not infringe upon the copyright of another. However, you do have to quote your source.

✍ Never Plagiarize

Plagiarism—the act of using or passing off the ideas or writings of another as your own—can have serious repercussions. Many academic institutions, especially colleges and universities, treat plagiarism with the utmost severity. Some even permanently expel students for violations. Don't ever risk it—use citations where appropriate.

As you learned in Chapter 6, there are specific methods for citing material from other works when writing academic papers. However, if you aren't writing an academic paper, merely acknowledging the source should be sufficient. For example:

> According to Professor Bloggs of the University of Arkansonia's literary studies department, 37 percent of male teenagers like to read spy novels, while only 12 percent of the adult male population likes to read them.

Derivative Works

Copyright owners have the right to make derivative works. This is most obvious in the case of fiction, where fictional characters are cast in events to create a story. As long as a fictional character is sufficiently sketched out, it is a proper object of copyright.

For instance, you couldn't use the Harry Potter characters in your own work without permission.

The right to create derivative works also encompasses the creation of other forms of work based on the original, such as movies or TV shows or even merchandise bearing characters' likenesses. For years after the death of Sir Arthur Conan Doyle, anyone who wanted to use the Sherlock Holmes character had to have permission from the author's estate. As an author, use of your fictional characters is protected, but by the same token, you must also take care not to violate the copyright of others.

Copyright Notices

Even though a notice of copyright is no longer required for a claim to be supported, it is still a good idea to include it. Some writers argue that because copyright exists once a work is saved to a reproducible medium, such copyright is always implied. However, one of the defenses to an accusation of copyright infringement is lack of knowledge that copyright existed in the work. That defense is not applicable if the work bears a copyright notice. Therefore, a copyright notice is an author's best protection.

Although the word and symbol are often used together, for a proper copyright notice, it is really only necessary to include either the word "copyright" or its symbol, a small "c" with a circle around it (e.g., ©). It should also bear the date of creation. And, unless the author or owner of the work is clear elsewhere in the context of the manuscript, the copyright notice should also bear the name of the author or owner of the copyright. Positioning your notice close to the title is always a good bet.

Proof of Ownership

The chances of someone stealing your material are very, very slim. It does happen, but not to the extreme extent that beginning writers sometimes suspect. If you keep careful records of your work, you shouldn't have any problem. Keep records of where and when you submit your material, and any response you receive.

If you have a good story, and you want to be sure your work is protected, you can register it with the copyright office. You'll have to send in an application form, the required fee, and a copy of the work. The Library of Congress retains a copy of all registered copyrighted material, whether published or not. Depending on your particular circumstances, you may have to submit two or more copies instead of one. You can get all the details you need by contacting the federal government's copyright office at: Library of Congress, Copyright Office, 101 Independence Avenue, S.E., Washington, D.C. 20559-6000, Phone: (202) 707-3000, *www.copyright.gov.*

✍ Proper Documentation

The copyright symbol © has a special legal meaning. People sometimes use a small c surrounded by parenthesis, as in (c), but this does not have the same legal meaning. The only acceptable alternative to the © symbol is spelling the word "copyright" out in full. Just remember this handy copyright notice phrase: If in doubt, spell it out.

Chapter 14

What to Do When You Have Writer's Block

What happens when, despite your best efforts, the daunting threat of the blank page looms large, and you can't figure out how to conquer your writer's block? Maybe you're bored with your topic; maybe you started out strong, but suddenly find you're running out of steam. Writer's block strikes for lots of reasons—even the most gifted writers hit this stumbling block sometimes. When you're stumped by writer's block, don't panic or feel intimidated at the thought of forging ahead. You just need to learn how to write through your blocks, that's all. This quick wrapup chapter will present some useful tips to add to your bag of creative tricks, so that you can get yourself back on the road to writing when the going gets tough.

Lead with Your Best Shot

Your lead is your bait—the carrot you dangle in front of your reader. A good lead entices the reader and makes him or her want to read more.

A good lead can act as your incentive, too, by enticing you to want to write more. Sometimes, something as simple as rewriting your lead can jumpstart your productivity and get you back on track.

Sample Uninspiring Lead

Chronic Fatigue Syndrome and fibromyalgia advocate Pamela Rice Hahn spoke to the Celina Chamber of Commerce last night about things local businesses can do to help make shopping a friendlier experience for those in the community who suffer from illnesses or deal with disabilities.

Sample Lead, Rewritten as a "Visual" Lead

With slow, deliberate movements, the woman—her ankles swollen, her dress a bit too tight across her wide hips—lumbered to the podium. Facing the audience, she took a deep breath and said, "In a nation that celebrates physical fitness and supermodel beauties, it's difficult for someone with challenges like mine to be taken seriously. You see: I don't look sick; I just look fat." Thus began what proved to be an hour-long, insightful speech by author and Chronic Fatigue Syndrome and fibromyalgia advocate Pamela Rice Hahn.

Edit Out Problems

Sometimes, your subconscious (or conscious) can do a number on you. Maybe you've written something that although accurate could make readers uncomfortable or introduce unnecessary controversy into your piece. At other times, your editing issues might be less severe—for instance, you're concerned about overly long descriptions, verbose passages, or words that don't sound quite right. These sorts of problems don't just distract readers, they can preoccupy you to the point where writer's block kicks in.

✍ *Perfectionism Equals Procrastination*

Perfectionism is a form of procrastination. Don't get hung up on making every word sound perfect, if that's keeping you from completing your assignment. You want your writing to be the best it can be, but you don't want editing to become your excuse for not finishing.

If you suspect that might be the case, read over what you've written thus far and highlight or underline any passages that don't sit well with you. (It isn't necessary at this point to make a decision as to whether or not you should cut or replace those passages. This exercise is supposed to make them stand out so that you'll remember to address those issues when you polish your final draft.)

> With slow, deliberate movements, the woman—<u>her ankles swollen, her dress a bit too tight across her wide hips</u>—lumbered to the podium. Facing the audience, she took a deep breath and said, "In a nation that celebrates physical fitness and supermodel beauties, it's difficult for someone with challenges like mine to be taken seriously. You see: I don't look sick; I just look fat." Thus began <u>what proved to be an hour-long, insightful</u> speech by author and Chronic Fatigue Syndrome and fibromyalgia advocate Pamela Rice Hahn.

Fill in the Blanks Later

When you write an initial draft, your first order of business is simply "getting your story down." That's tough to do if you keep interrupting yourself to look up facts or rack your brain for the perfect word. Steer clear of writing flow disruptions by inserting a place marker into your paragraphs so that you'll know where you'll need to refer back to and rewrite later on.

> Shortly before leaving the office, in a January 2002 press release Surgeon General Dr. David Satcher put the number of people diagnosed with Chronic Fatigue Syndrome at one million. The local health department estimates that number locally is ***xxx, with another ***xxx locally who must cope with other disabling conditions like MS and arthritis.

Hone Your Outline

If you're still struggling with what shape your writing should take, there are things you can do to develop your outline further. One method is to pick a word or term specific to your topic and write out its definition. Then do another definition. Starting with the simplest, more elementary terms and progressing to the more complex ideas, place those terms in the order you think they should be introduced in your paper.

For longer works, like a novel, chances are you have some idea about scenes you plan to include. With a romance, for example, write up the first meeting and first kiss scenes. Perhaps write another scene that includes a description of one of the places where your hero and heroine will spend time. Once you've written several scenes, decide where they fit into the book's overall story, and write your outline around those scenes.

Generating Ideas

One of the most common questions asked of writers is: "Where do you get your ideas?" Some authors get frustrated with that question, because the simple answer is: All over the place! (In fact, once you begin writing on a daily basis, you might eventually ask yourself, "How do I get the ideas to stop long enough so I can decide which one I want to write about next?")

The simple trick is to be open to ideas as they come along. Your imagination is like a muscle. The more you allow your imagination to play, the more adept it will become at generating interesting ideas.

Immediate Ideas

There are a variety of tricks you can use to cultivate short-term ideas. The following list provides just some examples. Remember, the more you play, the more you're likely to come up with ideas that work for you. As mentioned above, the trick is to be open to ideas as they come along.

On the Bus or Train

As you ride around waiting to get to your destination, covertly observe others around you. Where might they be going? What kind of mood are they in? What kind of story can you weave about them? Come up with a history of how they got there and what they are doing. What are they wearing? Are they dressed shabbily or immaculately? Do you think that any of the people on the bus actually know each other, but are pretending not to for some strange reason? Use these details as a springboard, and let your imagination run wild. All of these questions can give you insights and ideas for characters that you can use in your own stories.

✍ Partial Ideas

There is no set formula for generating story ideas, and ideas don't always hit you all at once. Sometimes, you'll get a partial idea, and then a few days later, a slightly different idea will come along. Your subconscious may combine the two and come up with an innovative third idea you'll just love, and that could get you motivated to write.

In the News

What's happening in your community, across the country, and around the world? One small element in a news story or a human interest feature can spark wonderful ideas. Keep a notepad beside you and jot down ideas as they come to you. Play a game, and pull one element from one story (such as a break-in at the doughnut shop) and combine it with an element from another story (like a little old lady who purchased a winning lottery ticket). How can you combine these into an interesting story?

On Your Bookshelf

Do the same thing with the books on your bookshelf. Flip through and look for details that trigger your imagination. Sometimes, a short phrase is enough to do the trick. Just pick a page at random and see what lies there waiting for you. Any book works, too. Who knows? A book on prescription drugs might give you a great idea for a murder mystery.

On Television

This can work, too, but be careful with it. You don't want to get too caught up in what you're watching. Grab your remote, and flip through channels at random. Maybe a champagne ice bucket you see on the shopping channel will give you an idea. Combine that bucket with the tube of lipstick you see a couple of channels later, and notions of smeared lipstick and a little too much champagne could help you to conjure the image of a late evening after a celebration.

The Yellow Pages

Sure, it seems absurd, but the Yellow Pages offer a concise encyclopedia of the businesses and services that are available in your area. Each one is a potential idea for the location of a story. If you're having trouble coming up with names for your characters, try the phone book. There's a big list of names there. Choose a first name from one page, then choose a last name from a different page. Just be careful to pick and choose, and not name your characters after someone who already exists.

Long-Term Ideas

Long-term ideas are really just an extension of short-term idea generating strategies. The only trick is to come up with some way to remember what all of these ideas are when you don't have time to work on them. Using the story-generating ideas in the short-term section, you'll soon find that you'll have more ideas than you know what to do with.

Keep an ideas folder. When ideas hit you, write them down. Whether you write your ideas on scraps of paper and keep them in a file folder, or you use a notebook expressly for that purpose, if you record ideas at the time they strike you, they'll be there waiting for you when you need them. Never count on your memory when it comes to story ideas, because they tend to be fleeting things that disappear if they don't get used.

Sample: Bad Notes

Ice cream parlor—chocolate sprinkles

While the above example might give you enough to recall the idea a few days later, as time wears on, you'll forget the details you didn't write down. If your notes are more extensive, chances are you'll be able to recall the entire scene, or at least be able to reconstruct it.

Sample: Good Notes

> Flashback: Little girl—ice cream parlor—got money from grandmother to buy a cone—wants chocolate sprinkles—doesn't have enough money—nice old gentleman gives her extra nickel—affects little girl for rest of life—she becomes compassionate remembering the kindness of old man who helped her.

Your ideas folder can also contain copies of magazine articles or newspaper clippings, but you may also want to attach a sheet outlining why this piece spoke to you and what kind of ideas it gave to you. Write down everything you can in your notes. Personal observations, snippets of conversations you have overheard, and impressions about setting and mood are all important things to record. If you have ideas for dialog, it's a good idea to elaborate on that in your notes. That way, your dialog will have context, and you'll have an idea later about how you wanted to use the quotes.

Commit yourself to maintaining these notes, and you'll always have a resource to consult when you're stuck for ideas.

A Few More Helpful Hints

Writing deadlines can be stressful, and it's easy to overlook the obvious when you're under that kind of pressure. Here are some other things you can do to get beyond writer's block:

- Break up your writing assignment into a series of tasks; promise yourself some sort of reward each time you complete one.
- Decide you need to get the job done, and just start typing.
- Make sure you understand the assignment.
- Talk to yourself. (Pretend you're verbally explaining your topic to somebody and write down what you say.)
- Write the ending first. This way, when you go back to the beginning and start writing your paper, the end really will be "in sight."

The most important thing to remember when writer's block hits you is that it's not a fatal affliction. It's just an indication that your mind is temporarily playing tricks on you and, for whatever reason, is trying to interfere with your productivity. If you try one exercise to overcome your block and it doesn't work, don't give up. Just try another—eventually, something is bound to work. Writing is like any other worthwhile endeavor: Persistence pays off. Stick to it, and you'll reap the rewards of a job well done.

Index